GRACE BEYOND DIVORCE

"Marriage, Divorce, and Remarriage in God's Redemption Plan"

Copyright © 2025 by **Dr. Jean Héder Petit Frère**

All rights reserved. No part of this book may be reproduced, stored in a retrieval system, or transmitted in any form or by any means electronic, mechanical, photocopying, recording, or otherwise–without the prior written permission of the publisher, except in the case of brief quotations in critical articles or reviews.

Scripture quotations are taken from the Holy Bible. Unless otherwise noted, Scripture quotations are from the King James Version (KJV). Other versions used include the New International Version (NIV), English Standard Version (ESV), and others, credited where applicable.

This book is intended as a resource for biblical teaching and pastoral guidance. It is not a substitute for professional counseling, legal advice, or therapy. Readers are encouraged to seek appropriate counsel for personal situations.

Published by:
Kingdom Records Unlimited
P.O. Box 560468
Orlando, FL 32856, USA

Printed in the United States of America

ISBN: 978-1-7353215-1-6 All rights reserved worldwide.

Contents

Part I	23
Foundations Of Covenant	23
Chapter 1	25
God's Original Design for Marriage	25
A Divine Blueprint: Rediscovering the Sacred Foundations of Marriage	25
Marriage as God's Idea, Not Man's	25
The Spiritual Dimension of Marriage	28
Chapter 2	31
When Covenant Breaks	31
Shattered Vows: Understanding the Consequences of Broken Promises	31
The First Mention of Divorce	31
The Violence of Broken Covenant	34
Chapter 3	41
Divorce in the Law of Moses	41
Regulation and Redemption: Unpacking Mosaic Divorce Provisions	41
The Heart of the Question	42
The Example of God's Own Covenant with Israel	44
The Ripple Effect of Divorce in Israel	45
Closing Reflection	48
Chapter 4	51
Jesus' Teaching on Divorce	51
Restoring God's Ideal: The Radical Call of Christ on Marriage and Divorce	51

The Sermon on the Mount: Raising the Standard	52
The Mirror of Christ and the Church	56
Prophetic Warning for Today	58
Conclusion: The Standard of the Kingdom	58
Chapter 5	59
Paul's Teaching on Divorce	59
Paul's Counsel on Separation and Reconciliation	59
Faithfulness Among Believers	60
Paul's Pastoral Balance	64
Prophetic Insight: Covenant and Peace	66
Closing Reflection	67
Part II	69
When Covenant Breaks	69
Chapter 6	71
Abuse, Neglect, and Covenant Violation	71
When the Covenant Is Broken: Addressing Abuse and Neglect in Marriage	71
Physical Abuse: Violence Against One's Own Flesh	72
Verbal and Emotional Abuse: Wounds Without Scars	76
God Has Called Us to Peace	81
The Role of the Church: Shepherd or Silent Partner?	84
Forgiveness and Restoration	86
Chapter 7	91
The Shattered Home: The Impact of Divorce on Children, Community, and Nations	91
Echoes Beyond the Home	91
The Impact on Children: Silent Casualties of Broken Covenants	92
The Impact on Families: Ripples Through Generations	94
The Impact on Communities: Broken Homes, Broken Streets	97
The Impact on Nations: Foundations Shaken	99

Divorce as Spiritual Warfare	101
The Church's Prophetic Responsibility	103
Chapter 8	107
Family Altars and Generational Curses in Marriage	107
Heritage and Bondage	107
What Are Family Altars?	108
How Family Altars Affect Marriage	109
How to Identify Family Altars	113
Building a Godly Family Altar	117
Part III	121
Healing And Restoration	121
Chapter 9	123
Questions of Remarriage	123
Navigating Second Chances and Sacred Boundaries	123
When Covenant Ends	124
When Remarriage Becomes Adultery	125
Grace and Responsibility	128
Closing Reflection	130
Chapter 10	133
Boundaries, Forgiveness, and Restoration	133
Rebuilding Trust on the Road to Wholeness	133
Why Boundaries Matter in Covenant Love	133
Common Boundaries That Protect Marriage	137
When Boundaries Are Violated	138
The Nature of Forgiveness	140
Forgiveness Versus Restoration	141
When Forgiveness Is Not Enough	142
The Prophetic Role of Boundaries and Forgiveness	143
Closing Reflection	144
Chapter 11	147
The Role of the Church as a Healing Community	147
Embracing the Broken and Restoring Hope	147

The Church as Covenant Witness	149
Shepherding Through Marital Crisis	151
The Church as Family for the Fatherless	153
The Tension of Truth and Grace	155
Divorce, Remarriage, and Ministry	156
Closing Reflection	157
Chapter 12	159
Questions and Objections People Raise About Divorce and Remarriage	159
Clarifying Concerns in Light of Scripture	159
Must I Leave My New Spouse and Return to My First?	159
Conclusion: Grace Greater Than Our Questions	163
Chapter 13	165
Healing After Divorce: Personal, Spiritual, and Relational Renewal	165
Hope Restored	165
Personal Healing: Facing the Wound Honestly	166
Rebuilding Trust with God and with Self	168
The Role of the Church in Healing	168
Closing Reflection	169
Chapter 14	171
Rebuilding Life and Purpose After Divorce	171
"Finding Meaning Beyond the Pain	171
Rediscovering Who You Are	172
Rebuilding Daily Life	176
Rebuilding Family	178
Rebuilding Finances	180
Rebuilding Calling and Ministry	182
Prophetic Vision for the Future	186
Final Word	188
Part IV	191
Closing Word	191
From Ashes to Beauty	193
A Prophetic Prayer and Charge	197

DEDICATION

To every man and woman who has sat in silence with tears no one saw,
to every child caught in the storm of broken vows,
to every pastor who has quietly felt disqualified by popular but uninformed opinions,
to every believer who has endured whispers of judgment instead of words of grace,
to all who are still struggling in a marriage that feels like a prison with no light of change in sight,
to those who have wasted what feels like an entire lifetime in a broken relationship for lack of revelation,
to the widowed in spirit though not in law,
to those abandoned in body or in heart,
to the shamed, the scarred, and the silenced,
to the faithful who fought but still lost,
and to the weary who wonder if they will ever know joy again –This book is for you.

May you discover that grace is greater than failure,
that redemption is stronger than regret,
that your scars can become testimonies,
and that the God of covenant is also the God of restoration.

Acknowledgments

First and foremost, I give glory and honor to the Lord Jesus Christ, the Bridegroom who never breaks covenant, and the Holy Spirit, who has carried me through every page of this work. Without His grace, revelation, and mercy, this book would not exist.

To my beloved wife, Marcia Elaine, and to our children, Sara and her husband, Junior; Jason, Hannah, and Matthew: you are my greatest earthly blessings. Thank you for your patience, your encouragement, and your unwavering belief in the calling God has placed upon my life. This book bears your fingerprints, for your love and your sacrifices have been the silent backdrop to every word.

To my extended family and my spiritual family across Haiti, Canada, and the United States, you have been both soil and seed for this message. Your testimonies, struggles, and faith have shaped me more than I can express.

To my fellow pastors, leaders, and shepherds, many of you have carried hidden pain, unanswered questions, and burdens unspoken. Some of you have felt disqualified by the uninformed opinions of others. Your courage and perseverance inspired me to speak into silence. This book is a tribute to your faithfulness.

To the countless men and women who have shared their stories with me over the years in counseling sessions, church pews, late-night calls, or whispered conversations after services, you may not realize it, but your tears watered these pages. Your questions, your honesty, and even your silence gave me the conviction to write. I thank you for trusting me with your brokenness.

To those who, while carrying their own wounds, have still chosen to counsel others, intercede for them, and make themselves available as vessels of comfort, you are the hidden heroes. You embody Christ, the wounded Healer, who carried our sorrows while bearing His own. Your sacrifice has carried many through storms and has left an invisible yet eternal mark on this work.

To those who still live in the shadow of marriages that have not healed, who have wasted what feels like decades without revelation, who fight daily battles behind closed doors – your perseverance is seen by heaven.

To those who struggle daily with unseen forces that war against their marriages' spiritual strongholds, generational patterns, cultural pressures, or relentless attacks from the enemy, your battle has not gone unnoticed. Your endurance, even in weakness, is a testimony that hell cannot erase. May this book remind you that you are not fighting alone and that the God of covenant is fighting for you.

Finally, I acknowledge every intercessor, friend, and partner in ministry who stood with me, encouraged me, and prayed me through this project. Your faithfulness is a gift I will never take lightly.

This book is not the work of one man's pen, but the fruit of many lives, many voices, and above all, God's unrelenting grace. To each of you, I say: thank you.

PREFACE

Divorce is one of the most painful realities of our time. It cuts deeply into families, communities, and nations. It raises difficult questions: *Does God permit divorce? What about abuse, neglect, or abandonment? Is remarriage possible, and if so, when? What role does the church play in shepherding the divorced and the remarried?*

For too long, the church has often swung between two extremes: harsh legalism that offers no compassion or careless permissiveness that ignores God's standard. Both distort the heart of God. He is the covenant-keeping God who upholds holiness, yet He is also the Redeemer who binds up the brokenhearted.

This book is my attempt to walk the narrow road between those two extremes: to honor God's high view of marriage while extending His mercy to those scarred by divorce. But it is also more than a book about marriage and divorce. It is a prophetic call to recognize the **hidden family altars and generational curses** that often sabotage relationships without our awareness. Unless these spiritual roots are dealt with, many will repeat cycles of brokenness across generations.

What you hold in your hands is not only a theological study but also **a healing manual and prophetic guide.** It is written for pastors and leaders who counsel God's people, for believers wrestling with painful questions, for couples seeking to build marriages on the rocks, and for those who need restoration after a covenant has been broken.

My prayer is that as you read, you will hear both the **truth that sets free** and the **grace that heals.** May this work bring clarity where there is confusion, hope where there is despair, and courage where there is fear.

Introduction

Why We Must Talk About Divorce and Family Altars Today

We live in a world where marriage is under siege. Divorce rates climb, even among believers. Homes that should be places of safety are often places of pain. Children grow up carrying invisible scars. Nations collapse under the weight of broken families.

But beneath the visible struggles lies an invisible battle. Many marriages are not only strained by human weakness but also attacked by **spiritual altars and generational curses**. Unbroken cycles of infidelity, rejection, abuse, addiction, or poverty often reappear in family lines. A man swears he will never be like his abusive father, yet years later his wife bears the same wounds his mother carried. A woman longs for stability, yet chooses partners who repeat the instability of her upbringing. These are not coincidences; they are **family altars** still crying out until someone confronts them in Christ.

This is why the topic of divorce cannot be addressed merely as a legal or moral issue. It must also be addressed as a **covenant and altar issue**. If we ignore the spiritual roots, we will only treat the surface. If we deal with the altars, however, we can bring true deliverance and restoration.

In this book, we will:

Return to God's original design for marriage.

Study what the Bible truly says about divorce and remarriage.

Expose the hidden family altars that destroy relationships.

Equip pastors and leaders to shepherd wisely.

Offer healing, hope, and restoration for those scarred by divorce.

This is not a book of condemnation but of **redemption.** It is not a book of opinions but of **biblical truth and prophetic insight.** Above all, it is a book of **hope**—because while covenants may be broken, God is still able to heal, restore, and give beauty for ashes.

PART I

FOUNDATIONS OF COVENANT

CHAPTER 1

God's Original Design for Marriage

A Divine Blueprint: Rediscovering the Sacred Foundations of Marriage

Before we can talk about divorce, remarriage, or family altars, we must first go back to the beginning. For without understanding **God's original design**, we cannot truly understand the tragedy of divorce nor the hope of restoration.

MARRIAGE AS GOD'S IDEA, NOT MAN'S

Marriage was not invented by culture, nor imposed by religion. It was born in the heart of God. In the opening chapters of Genesis, long before there was sin, pain, or brokenness, God Himself declared: *"It is not good that the man should be alone; I will make him a helper fit for him."* (Genesis 2:18)

Adam had communion with God, authority over creation, and the freedom of Eden, yet something was incomplete. God saw what Adam could not articulate: that man was created for covenantal companionship. And so God formed Eve, not from the dust as He did Adam, but from Adam's rib bone, bone of his bone, and flesh of his flesh (Gen 2:21–23).

This was not merely biology. It was prophecy. By taking woman out of man and then bringing her back to him in covenant, God was showing that **marriage is the reuniting of what was separated, two becoming one again.**

THE COVENANT DIMENSION

Genesis 2:24 gives us the foundation: *"Therefore a man shall leave his father and mother and be joined to his wife, and they shall become one flesh."*

Here we see three pillars:

Leaving: a shift in loyalty from parents to spouse.

Cleaving: a permanent joining, like two pieces of wood fused together.

Becoming one flesh: not only physical intimacy, but spiritual and covenantal union.

Marriage is therefore more than romance, more than partnership, and more than contract. It is a **covenant.** Additionally, God Himself has testified that a covenant is sacred (Malachi 2:14). It is not just between husband and wife but between them and God.

CHRIST AND THE CHURCH: THE ULTIMATE MODEL

The Apostle Paul takes this further in Ephesians 5:31–32: *"For this reason a man shall leave his father and mother and be joined to his wife, and the two shall become one flesh. This is a profound mystery—but I am talking about Christ and the church."*

Marriage was never only about Adam and Eve, or you and your spouse. It was always pointing to the greater reality of Christ the Bridegroom and His Bride, the Church.

Just as Christ left His Father's side to win His bride, so the man leaves his parents.

Just as Christ cleaves to His church in faithfulness, so the husband must cleave to his wife.

Just as Christ and His church are united as one body, so husband and wife become one flesh.

This means marriage is not only **personal** but also **prophetic.** When a marriage flourishes, it preaches the gospel without words. When a marriage breaks, it distorts the picture of Christ and His Bride.

WHY GOD HATES DIVORCE

In Malachi 2:16, God declares, *"I hate divorce."* Why such strong language?

Because divorce is **covenant-breaking.** It tears apart what God has joined.

Because divorce is **violent.** Malachi calls it "covering one's garment with violence." It leaves scars not only on the spouses but also on children and families.

Because divorce is **a false testimony.** If marriage is meant to mirror Christ and His church, divorce distorts that mirror.

But notice: God does not say He hates divorced people. He hates the act because of the damage it causes, but he loves the people caught in its pain. His hatred of divorce is really an expression of His love for His children.

THE SPIRITUAL DIMENSION OF MARRIAGE

From the beginning, Satan has attacked marriages. Why? Because marriage is the **first human covenant** and the foundation of society. Destroy the marriage, and you weaken the family. Destroy the family, and you unravel the nation.

In Eden, Satan targeted Eve to fracture the covenant.

Today, he still seeks to break homes through infidelity, abuse, neglect, and hidden altars.

This is why many couples struggle with patterns they did not create; generational cycles of divorce, unfaithfulness, or rejection. These are often signs of **family altars** at work. We will explore this more in Chapter 3, but for now understand: marriage is not only relational, it is **spiritual warfare.**

PRACTICAL ILLUSTRATION

I once counseled a couple who loved each other dearly, yet they could not stop fighting. Every small issue escalated into war. As we prayed, the Lord revealed that both came from generations of broken marriages. His father had left his mother; her parents had divorced after years of bitterness. Neither wanted to repeat the past, yet without realizing it, they were walking in the same patterns.

When they renounced those family altars in prayer and built a new altar of worship together in their home, peace began to reign. Their marriage didn't become perfect overnight, but the cycle was broken. This is why understanding God's design is so critical: it empowers us to see where the enemy has twisted it and how Christ restores it.

Reflection Questions

How does seeing marriage as a covenant (not just a contract) change your perspective?

In what ways does your marriage reflect Christ and the church—and in what areas does it struggle?

Do you see patterns from your family line that may still affect your relationships today?

Declaration

I declare that marriage is God's covenant, not man's idea. I shall uphold the covenant of marriage as a representation of Christ and His church. I disagree with generational trends of divorce, unfaithfulness, and rejection. My family will not rebuild the old altars; instead, we will build a new altar of covenant and worship in Christ.

Prayer

Father, thank You for designing marriage as a covenant and not just a contract. Forgive us where we have treated it lightly. Lord, expose the hidden altars in our families that war against our relationships. Help us to walk in the unity, love, and covenant faithfulness that reflect Christ and His church. May our marriages preach the gospel without words, bringing glory to You and hope to a broken world. In Jesus' name, amen.

Let's move into **Chapter 2**. This chapter will carry more weight, because here we deal with the painful reality of broken covenant—why God permitted divorce under Moses, what "hardness of heart" means, and how it still affects marriages today.

CHAPTER 2

WHEN COVENANT BREAKS

Shattered Vows: Understanding the Consequences of Broken Promises

MARRIAGE WAS CREATED IN EDEN. Divorce was born in brokenness. Divorce is never God's original plan, but Scripture does acknowledge its reality. To understand it, we must see both the **biblical permission** and the **human hardness** behind it. Divorce is a painful and complex topic that many people face in their lives. It is important to approach the issue with sensitivity and understanding, while also seeking wisdom and guidance from God's word. As we delve into Chapter 2, we will explore the reasons behind divorce and how we can navigate through the brokenness with faith and grace. Let us open our hearts and minds to the truth, seeking healing and restoration in God's love.

THE FIRST MENTION OF DIVORCE

The first time divorce is formally addressed in Scripture is in **Deuteronomy 24:1–4**: *"When a man takes a wife and marries her, if* *then she finds no favor in his eyes because he has found some indecency in her, and he writes her a certificate of divorce and puts it in her hand and sends her out of his house, and she departs out of his house, and if she goes and becomes another man's wife, and the latter man hates her and writes her a certificate of divorce and puts it in her hand... then her former husband, who sent her away, may not take her again to be his wife after she has been defiled."*

Here, divorce is not commanded—it is **regulated**. God, through Moses, set boundaries around a practice that was already happening. He insisted on:

A **written certificate** (to protect the woman from being discarded without proof).

A **prohibition against returning to the first husband** after a second marriage (to prevent legal "wife-swapping" and treating marriage lightly).

This shows us a critical truth: **divorce was never God's will, but His concession.** Divorce was allowed as a way to protect women from unjust treatment and to maintain order within society. By setting guidelines for divorce, God was ensuring that the sanctity of marriage was upheld and that individuals were held accountable for their actions. It is clear that God's ultimate desire is for marriages to be strong and lasting, but He also understands the complexities of human relationships and provides a way out when necessary. Marriage is a sacred institution that should not be taken lightly, and divorce should be seen as a last resort rather than a quick solution to marital problems.

WHY DID GOD ALLOW IT?

Jesus Himself answers this in **Matthew 19:8**: *"Because of your hardness of heart, Moses allowed you to divorce your wives, but from the beginning it was not so."*

Two key insights here:

Hardness of heart: a stubborn, unrepentant spirit that refuses God's way. Divorce is the tragic result when cruelty, betrayal, or indifference replace covenant love. Divorce should not be taken lightly because it goes against the sacred covenant of marriage. When couples allow their hearts to harden and refuse to repent and seek God's guidance, the marriage is at risk of falling apart. Instead of resorting to divorce as a quick fix, couples should strive to work through their issues with love, forgiveness, and a willingness to change. In doing so, they can honor the sanctity of marriage and strengthen their relationship for the long haul.

It was not so from the beginning: divorce was never in God's Eden design. Marriage was meant to be a lifelong covenant. Divorce exists only because of sin. When couples make the commitment to work through their problems together, they are choosing to uphold the sacred bond of marriage that God intended. By showing love, forgiveness, and a willingness to change, they are honoring their vows and demonstrating their faith in each other. While divorce may be a reality in today's world, it is not the ideal outcome for a marriage that is built on a foundation of love and commitment. Couples who choose to fight for their relationship and seek God's guidance can find strength and healing in their marriage, despite the challenges they may face.

Think of it like this: divorce is like an emergency exit. God placed it there because He knew human hearts would grow hard, but His desire is always that no one has to use it.

THE RABBINIC DEBATE: HILLEL VS. SHAMMAI

By the time of Jesus, Jewish teachers debated Deuteronomy 24 fiercely.

Rabbi Shammai taught that "indecency" (Hebrew: *ervah*) meant sexual immorality only. Strict view.

Rabbi Hillel taught that "indecency" could be anything displeasing, even burning the dinner! Very permissive.

Most people preferred Hillel's easier path. But when asked, Jesus sided with Shammai and then raised the standard even higher: *"Whoever divorces his wife, except for sexual immorality, and marries another, commits adultery."* (Matt 19:9)

Jesus restored God's original intent: divorce only in cases of covenant-breaking, not for trivial reasons.

THE VIOLENCE OF BROKEN COVENANT

Malachi 2:13–16 exposes the deeper tragedy: *"The LORD was witness between you and the wife of your youth, to whom you have been faithless... For the man who does not love his wife but divorces her... covers his garment with violence, says the LORD of hosts."*

In God's eyes, divorce is not just separation—it is violence. Not necessarily physical violence, but covenant violence. It tears apart what was joined. It wounds children, destabilizes families, and weakens the community. Divorce, in God's eyes, is a breaking of a sacred promise and a betrayal of the covenant made between two individuals. It is a form of violence that not only impacts the couple involved but also has ripple effects on their children, families, and the broader community. By emphasizing the seriousness of divorce as a form of violence,

Malachi reminds us of the importance of honoring our commitments and treating our relationships with the utmost respect and care.

Divorce is **violent to the spouse** who is abandoned.

Divorce is **violent to children** who lose the stability of covenant love.

Divorce is **violent to society** because strong nations are built on strong families.

HARDNESS OF HEART IN OUR TIME

Hardness of heart is still the root of many divorces today.

A husband refuses to repent of pornography. He neglects his wife's emotional needs and seeks fulfillment outside of their marriage, causing irreparable damage to their relationship. The wife, feeling unloved and unwanted, begins to withdraw and eventually seeks solace in the arms of another man. The children witness their parents' crumbling marriage and are left feeling confused, hurt, and abandoned. The cycle of violence continues as the family unit disintegrates, leaving a trail of devastation in its wake. It is only through recognizing the harmful effects of divorce and addressing the root causes of marital breakdown that we can begin to heal and rebuild our relationships for the betterment of ourselves, our families, and our society as a whole.

A wife nurtures bitterness until it poisons love. As a result of his guilt and shame, the husband descends even further into rage and resentment.

The once happy home is now filled with tension and hostility, creating a toxic environment for all involved. As the wife seeks comfort in the arms of another man, the husband's heart hardens, closing off any chance for reconciliation. The children, caught in the middle, struggle to make sense of the chaos around them, longing for the stability and love that once filled their home. Only by facing their own demons and working towards forgiveness and understanding can this family begin to mend the broken pieces and move forward towards a brighter future.

Couples refuse counseling or accountability, only prolonging the pain and resentment that has built up over time. It is only through open communication and a willingness to address their issues head-on that this family can hope to heal and rebuild trust. Without taking these crucial steps, the cycle of hurt and betrayal will continue to poison their relationships, leaving them trapped in a cycle of dysfunction and despair. It is up to each individual to take responsibility for their actions and make the necessary changes to create a more positive and harmonious environment for themselves and their loved ones. Only then can they truly begin to heal and move forward towards a brighter future.

Pride keeps both parties from forgiveness. Forgiveness is a key component in breaking the cycle of hurt and betrayal. It requires humility and empathy to let go of past grievances and move towards reconciliation. By setting aside pride and focusing on understanding and compassion, both parties can begin the process of healing and rebuilding trust. It is important for each individual to recognize their own role in the conflict and take steps towards making amends and seeking forgiveness. Only through this commitment to change and growth can they truly break free from the cycle of dysfunction and despair.

When hearts remain hard, reconciliation becomes impossible. The covenant dies not because God's design failed, but because human hearts resisted His Spirit. When hearts remain closed off and unwilling to change, the cycle of dysfunction and despair will continue to persist. It is essential for both parties to humble themselves and allow God's Spirit to work in their hearts, guiding them towards reconciliation and healing. By acknowledging their own faults and seeking forgiveness, individuals can begin to break free from the barriers that have kept them from experiencing true peace and restoration. Ultimately, it is through God's grace and love that reconciliation can be achieved, despite the challenges and hurts that may have caused the rift in the first place.

ILLUSTRATION: THE WITHERED VINE

A marriage is like a vineyard. If watered with love, forgiveness, and prayer, it flourishes. But if left untended, weeds of resentment grow. The soil hardens, the vine withers, and eventually the fruit dies. Divorce is not the sudden frost–it is the slow hardening of the ground until life can no longer flow.

PASTORAL INSIGHT

As pastors, we must hold two tensions:

Uphold the sanctity of covenant. Do not trivialize divorce or present it as an easy option. We must also offer grace and compassion to those who are struggling in their marriages, recognizing that sometimes reconciliation is not possible. It is important to provide support and guidance to help couples navigate the difficult process of divorce with as much dignity and respect as possible. Ultimately, our goal should be to help heal the wounds caused by broken relationships and foster a sense of hope and renewal for the future.

Acknowledge the reality of brokenness. Some marriages are destroyed by adultery, violence, or abandonment. In such cases, pretending nothing is wrong only deepens the pain. Instead, we must confront the harsh truth of the situation and offer understanding to those who have faced such immense hurt. By acknowledging the reality of brokenness, we can begin the process of healing and moving forward in a healthy way. It is important to provide a safe space for individuals to express their pain and seek the support they need to rebuild their lives after such devastating experiences.

Our task is not to excuse sin nor to condemn the wounded, but to lead people into both repentance and restoration. Through this process of acknowledging and addressing the brokenness, we can foster a sense of hope and renewal in the lives of those affected. By offering compassion and support, we can help individuals navigate the difficult journey toward healing and reconciliation. It is only through facing the truth and extending grace that we can truly begin to mend the wounds caused by pain and betrayal. Let us commit to being a source of love and understanding for those who are struggling, guiding them towards a brighter future filled with healing and restoration.

Reflection Questions

Why did God permit divorce under Moses?
What does "hardness of heart" look like in modern marriages?
Have you seen divorce treated too lightly in society?
How can we restore God's standard while still showing mercy?

Declaration

I declare that my heart will not grow hard toward my spouse or toward God. I choose forgiveness over bitterness, humility over pride, and covenant faithfulness over selfishness. My marriage will be like a vineyard that has grace watering it rather than heartlessness choking it. I will seek guidance and wisdom from God to navigate any challenges that may arise in my marriage. I will strive to always show mercy and grace towards my spouse, even in difficult times. I believe that through prayer, communication, and a commitment to God's standard of love and faithfulness, my marriage can be a testament to His glory and grace. I declare that my heart will remain soft and open, allowing for healing and restoration to flow freely within my relationship.

Prayer

Lord, keep my heart soft before You and before my spouse. Protect me from pride, unforgiveness, and rebellion. Where covenant has been broken, bring repentance and healing. Where divorce has wounded, bring restoration and peace. May my life and marriage reflect Your covenant love, in Jesus' name, amen.

CHAPTER 3

Divorce in the Law of Moses

Regulation and Redemption: Unpacking Mosaic Divorce Provisions

When the subject of divorce arises in Scripture, most people instinctively turn to the words of Jesus in the Gospels or to Paul's instructions in the Epistles. But the story does not begin there. Long before the Sermon on the Mount or the letter to the Corinthians, the people of Israel were wrestling with the painful reality of broken marriages. The Mosaic Law itself speaks to divorce, and if we are to understand Jesus' teaching in its fullness, we must first understand what Moses wrote and why he wrote it. The laws regarding divorce in the time of Moses were quite different from what is commonly practiced today. In Deuteronomy 24:1-4, Moses allowed for a man to divorce his wife if he found "some indecency" in her. This was a controversial issue at the time, as some interpreted it as giving men too much power over their wives. However, the intent behind this law was to protect women from being abandoned without any means of support. Understanding the context and purpose of these laws is crucial in order to fully grasp the significance of Jesus' teachings on divorce.

THE HEART OF THE QUESTION

In **Deuteronomy 24:1–4**, we encounter one of the most debated passages in the Old Testament: *"When a man takes a wife and marries her, if then she finds no favor in his eyes because he has found some indecency in her, and he writes her a certificate of divorce and puts it in her hand and sends her out of his house, and she departs out of his house, and if she goes and becomes another man's wife, and the latter man hates her and writes her a certificate of divorce and puts it in her hand and sends her out of his house, or if the latter man dies who took her to be his wife, then her former husband, who sent her away, may not take her again to be his wife after she has been defiled, for that is an abomination before the Lord. And you shall not bring sin upon the land that the Lord your God is giving you for an inheritance."*

This passage, at first glance, seems to permit divorce. But upon closer study, it becomes clear that Moses is not endorsing divorce; he is **regulating** it. Divorce was already happening in Israel. Husbands were casting off their wives with little thought, leaving them destitute and dishonored. Women, who in that society often depended on their husbands for provision and legal standing, were left vulnerable, with no means of survival.

Moses intervened to provide **structure**. He commanded that if a man was going to dismiss his wife, he must give her a written certificate. This was not a celebration of divorce but a protection for the woman. That document gave her dignity and the ability to remarry without being treated as an adulteress. In other words, Moses was trying to **limit the damage of human sin**, not sanction it.

WHAT DID "SOME INDECENCY" MEAN?

The phrase "some indecency" (*'erwat dabar* in Hebrew) became the focal point of centuries of debate. Only sexual immorality met the criteria for "indecency," according to one school of rabbinic thought under Shammai. Another school, under the direction of Hillel, took it to mean that almost any complaint could justify divorce. Some rabbinic writings even suggest a husband could dismiss his wife if she spoiled his food or if he found another woman more attractive.

By the time of Jesus, this debate had created a permissive culture of divorce. The law of Moses, which was intended as a **fence against injustice**, had become a **loophole for selfishness.**

GOD'S TRUE HEART REVEALED IN MALACHI

Centuries after Moses, the prophet Malachi would thunder God's heart on the matter. In **Malachi 2:13–16**, the Lord accuses Israelite husbands of dealing "treacherously" with the wives of their youth: He condemns the practice of divorcing wives simply because they no longer found them pleasing, emphasizing the sacredness of the marriage covenant. God makes it clear that He hates divorce, as it goes against His original design for marriage to be a lifelong commitment based on love and faithfulness. The prophet Malachi's words serve as a powerful reminder to the Israelites, and to all believers, of the importance of honoring and cherishing the marriage relationship as a reflection of God's own covenantal love for His people.

> *"The Lord was witness between you and the wife of your youth, to whom you have been faithless, though she is your companion and your wife by covenant. Did He not make them one, with a portion of the Spirit in their union? ... For the man who does not love his wife but divorces her, says the Lord, the God of Israel, covers his garment with violence."*

Here, God uses strong words. Divorce, he says, is not a neutral legal act but an act of violence. It tears apart what He has joined, betrays covenant, and leaves scars that ripple across generations. The word "treachery" implies betrayal of trust, a covenantal breach that wounds both the victim and the covenant witness—God Himself.

THE EXAMPLE OF GOD'S OWN COVENANT WITH ISRAEL

The seriousness of covenant-breaking is underscored in the way God describes His relationship with Israel. In **Jeremiah 3:8**, God says, *"I gave faithless Israel her certificate of divorce and sent her away because of all her adulteries."* Even the Lord uses the metaphor of divorce to describe His painful decision to release His unfaithful people. But notice: His heart was never a final rejection. Through the prophets, He promises restoration, reconciliation, and a new covenant written on their hearts (Jer. 31:31–34).

If God Himself only "divorced" Israel after repeated, unrepentant betrayal, and even then longed for her return, it tells us much about His heart. Divorce is always a last resort, born not of God's will but of human rebellion. God's desire for His people is always reconciliation and restoration, even after the pain of betrayal. The metaphor of divorce is used to illustrate the severity of their unfaithfulness, but it is not the end of the story. God's love for Israel is unwavering, and His longing for their return is evident in His promises of a new covenant. This serves as a reminder that God's ultimate desire is to bring His people back to Him, despite their past mistakes.

DIVORCE AS CONCESSION, NOT COMMAND

When we read Moses' instructions, we must remember the distinction Jesus Himself made in Matthew 19:8: *"Because of your hardness of heart*

Moses allowed you to divorce your wives, but from the beginning it was not so." Divorce was a **concession**, not a command. It was God making space for a sinful people in a fallen world, much like His toleration of polygamy in the Old Testament. Neither was ever His ideal.

This distinction is vital. Some people use Moses' words as if they were a green light for divorce. In reality, they are more like a flashing warning sign: "Because of sin, this may happen. But do not mistake My tolerance for My desire."

A PASTORAL ILLUSTRATION: THE TEMPORARY FENCE

Imagine a farmer whose sheep keep straying into dangerous terrain. He builds a temporary fence to keep them from wandering too far. The fence is not his dream. His dream is that his sheep trust him and stay close. The fence is only a concession to their stubbornness. He knows that the fence is not the ideal situation, but it is necessary to protect his sheep from harm. In the same way, God's allowance for divorce in certain circumstances is not His ideal but a concession to the brokenness and sinfulness of humanity. God's desire is for marriages to be strong, loving, and lasting, just as the farmer's desire is for his sheep to stay close and trust him. The temporary fence serves as a reminder of the importance of staying faithful and committed in relationships, despite the challenges that may arise.

Moses' regulation of divorce was that fence. It was never God's dream. His dream has always been covenant faithfulness—one man, one woman, joined by Him, for life.

THE RIPPLE EFFECT OF DIVORCE IN ISRAEL

Even with Moses' regulation, divorce carried devastating effects in

Israelite society. Children were displaced, inheritances disrupted, and families fractured. Since property and lineage passed through fathers, divorce often left women and children without protection. Divorce was not merely a private tragedy; it became a public wound in the covenant community.

This is why Malachi warns that divorce "brings sin upon the land." When family covenants are broken, national stability is shaken. What happens at the altar of marriage eventually echoes in the gates of government.

PROPHETIC INSIGHT: DIVORCE AS A BROKEN ALTAR

Marriage is more than companionship. It is an altar where covenant is enacted and God's Spirit presides. To break it is not just to hurt another person—it is to desecrate an altar. This is why divorce leaves such deep scars. It is more than the ending of a relationship; it is the tearing down of a spiritual altar where God's presence once rested. Divorce is not just a personal matter but a societal one as well. The ripple effects of broken marriages can be felt in the fabric of a nation's moral foundation. When couples break their vows, it weakens the very structure of society. The sacredness of marriage is not just a human institution—it is a reflection of the covenant between God and His people. The consequences of divorce go far beyond the individuals involved; they impact the spiritual well-being of an entire community.

PRACTICAL IMPLICATIONS FOR TODAY

What does all this mean for us now?

We must never treat divorce lightly. It is not simply a "new chapter" but a tearing of covenant. Divorce should be approached with caution and with careful consideration of the consequences it may have on not only the individuals involved but also on the broader community. It is important to remember the sacredness of marriage and the commitment that comes with it. Instead of viewing divorce as an easy way out, we should strive to work through challenges and difficulties in our relationships, honoring the vows we made to each other and to God. By upholding the sanctity of marriage, we can contribute to the strength and stability of society as a whole.

We must protect the vulnerable. Just as Moses instituted certificates to protect women, the church today must ensure the abandoned, abused, and betrayed are not left defenseless. We must offer support and resources to those in unhealthy or dangerous marriages, encouraging them to seek help and find a safe way out if necessary. By providing a network of care and protection for the vulnerable, we can uphold the values of love, respect, and justice within our communities. It is our responsibility as a society to stand up against abuse and injustice and to advocate for the well-being and dignity of all individuals, especially those who are most in need of our protection. Only by standing together and supporting one another can we truly create a society that values and upholds the sanctity of marriage and the rights of all individuals.

We must preach God's heart, not human loopholes. The Law was not written to make divorce easy but to limit its damage. Our teaching should reflect that same priority. We must remember that marriage is a sacred commitment that should not be taken lightly. It is our duty to honor and uphold the vows we make to our partners and to work towards resolving conflicts and issues rather than seeking an easy way out through divorce. By promoting love, respect, and justice in our relationships and communities, we can create a world where all individuals are treated with dignity and compassion. Let us prioritize the well-being of all individuals, especially the most vulnerable among us, and strive to build a society that is built on the foundation of God's love and grace.

We must point people to redemption. Even when divorce happens, the story is not over. God longs to heal, restore, and even bring beauty from ashes. Let us not give up on each other or ourselves, but instead lean on God's strength and guidance to navigate the challenges that come our way. By choosing forgiveness and reconciliation, we can truly embody the values of love and grace that God has shown us. Let us remember that every individual has inherent worth and deserves a chance at redemption, no matter the circumstances. Let us be agents of healing and restoration in a world that so desperately needs it.

CLOSING REFLECTION

The Law of Moses was never meant to be the final word on marriage. It was a stopgap, a scaffold, a concession to brokenness. But within its limits, we see the faithfulness of God. He does not abandon the wounded. He provides even in our failure. Yet He also whispers, "This was not how it was meant to be."

As we turn from Moses to Jesus, we find not a relaxation of standards but a restoration of vision. Where Moses wrote to manage sin, Jesus came to transform hearts. Where Moses permitted because of hardness, Jesus empowers through grace. The Law was a shadow; Christ is the reality. Moses' prescription of marriage may have been a transient remedy for humanity's ills, but despite its limitations, we can still see God's unwavering faithfulness. Even in our failures and shortcomings, He remains steadfast and provides for us. However, in the transition from the Law of Moses to the teachings of Jesus, we are reminded that marriage was never meant to be a mere compromise. Jesus came not to lower the standards but to restore the original vision of what marriage should be–a union of two hearts transformed by grace and empowered to love unconditionally. In Him, we find the true reality of what marriage was always intended to be.

CHAPTER 4

Jesus' Teaching on Divorce

Restoring God's Ideal: The Radical Call of Christ on Marriage and Divorce

When Jesus spoke about divorce, He was stepping into a cultural storm. By the first century, marriage in Jewish society was in crisis. The Law of Moses had been interpreted and reinterpreted in ways that made divorce almost casual. Among the rabbis, the great debate was between two schools: **Shammai**, who insisted that divorce was permissible only for sexual immorality, and **Hillel**, who taught that a man could dismiss his wife for virtually any reason—even, according to some sources, if she burned his dinner or if he simply found another woman more pleasing. Jesus' teachings on divorce challenged the prevailing attitudes of His time. He emphasized the sanctity and permanence of marriage, stating that divorce should only be permitted in cases of adultery. This stricter stance caused controversy among the religious leaders of the day, but Jesus remained steadfast in His message of honoring the commitment made in marriage. His teachings continue to serve as a reminder of the importance of faithfulness and respect within the marital relationship.

This was the backdrop when Jesus began His ministry. Divorce was common. Women were discarded. Children were displaced. Covenant had been reduced to contract, and contracts could be canceled at will. Into this broken culture, Jesus' words came like a sword cutting through centuries of compromise. He spoke of the sacredness of marriage, reminding his followers that what God has joined together, let no one separate. His words challenged the societal norms of the time, calling for a higher standard of commitment and love within relationships. Despite the controversy and pushback he faced, Jesus continued to emphasize the importance of honoring the vows made in marriage and treating each other with respect and fidelity. His teachings on divorce and fidelity continue to be a powerful reminder for couples today to value and cherish their commitment to one another.

THE SERMON ON THE MOUNT: RAISING THE STANDARD

In **Matthew 5:31–32**, Jesus declares: *"It was also said, 'Whoever divorces his wife, let him give her a certificate of divorce.' But I say to you that everyone who divorces his wife, except on the ground of sexual immorality, makes her commit adultery, and whoever marries a divorced woman commits adultery."*

This was shocking. For generations, Jewish men had relied on the certificate of divorce from Deuteronomy 24 as a legal cover. As long as they had the paperwork, they considered themselves justified. But Jesus pierces through the paperwork to the **heart of** the covenant.

"You think the certificate protects you," he is saying. "But if you divorce for reasons other than sexual immorality, you are guilty of making your wife an adulteress, and the one who marries her shares in that guilt." In other words, divorce does not erase covenant. Paper does not nullify what God has joined.

This teaching was not just about law; it was about **love and holiness.** Jesus raises marriage back to its sacred place, where it was meant to be from the beginning.

THE PHARISEES' TEST IN MATTHEW 19

Later, in **Matthew 19:3–9**, the Pharisees confront Jesus directly: *"Is it lawful to divorce one's wife for any cause?"*

Notice the wording: *"for any cause."* They were baiting Him into the rabbinic debate. Would He side with Shammai's stricter view or Hillel's permissive one? But Jesus refuses to play their game. Instead of debating Deuteronomy, He takes them back to Genesis: *"Have you not read that He who created them from the beginning made them male and female and said, 'Therefore a man shall leave his father and his mother and hold fast to his wife, and the two shall become one flesh'? So they are no longer two but one flesh. What therefore God has joined together, let not man separate."* (vv. 4–6)

This is profound. Jesus bypasses centuries of argument and returns to the original design. Marriage is not primarily a legal contract but a **divine joining.** The man leaves. The woman cleaves. God Himself weaves them together into one flesh. And what God has joined, man has no right to tear apart. Marriage is a sacred union that goes beyond legalities and cultural norms. It is a spiritual bond that should be respected and honored. The idea of two individuals becoming one flesh is a beautiful and powerful concept that should not be taken lightly. When God brings two people together in marriage, it is a union that should be cherished and protected at all costs. It is a reminder of the love and commitment that should be shared between husband and wife.

When **pressed about Moses, Jesus explains:**

"Because of your hardness of heart Moses allowed you to divorce your wives, but from the beginning it was not so." (v. 8)

Here, Jesus makes the distinction we explored in the last chapter: divorce was a concession, not God's original design. It was tolerated because of sin, not celebrated as God's plan.

THE EXCEPTION CLAUSE: PORNEIA

Jesus does allow one exception: *"except for sexual immorality."* The Greek word used is "porneia"–broader than the term for adultery (*moicheia*). *"Porneia"* encompasses all forms of sexual immorality: fornication, prostitution, incest, homosexuality, and adultery. This exception clause indicates that divorce is permissible in cases of sexual immorality, as it goes against God's design for marriage. However, even in these instances, divorce should not be taken lightly and should be a last resort. It is clear from Jesus's teachings that marriage is a sacred union that should be honored and respected.

Why this exception? Because sexual unfaithfulness is not just a sin against the body; it is a desecration of the covenant itself. Marriage is built on exclusive intimacy, and when that exclusivity is shattered, the "one flesh" union is violently broken. Jesus does not command divorce in such cases, but He acknowledges that covenant has been compromised to the point where divorce is permitted.

Even then, grace still offers the possibility of forgiveness and restoration. But where repentance is absent or reconciliation rejected, divorce becomes a tragic but legitimate outcome.

THE DISCIPLES' SHOCK

The disciples respond in disbelief: *"If such is the case of a man with his wife, it is better not to marry."* (v. 10)

This shows just how radical Jesus' teaching was. In a culture where men assumed easy exits from marriage, the idea of a lifelong covenant with so few escape clauses sounded impossible. And that was precisely Jesus' point. Marriage is not to be entered lightly. It is a sacred covenant, not a convenient arrangement. Marriage requires commitment, sacrifice, and a willingness to work through challenges together. Jesus wanted to emphasize the importance of upholding the sanctity of marriage and the value of keeping one's promises. His teachings were meant to challenge the cultural norms of his time and encourage a deeper understanding of the true meaning of marriage as a lifelong bond between two individuals. The disciples' shock at Jesus' words serves as a reminder that marriage is a serious and sacred commitment that should not be taken lightly.

Jesus' words remind us that covenant love requires transformed hearts. Without grace, marriage feels impossible. With grace, it becomes a living parable of Christ and His church.

MARK AND LUKE'S EMPHASIS

In **Mark 10:11–12** and **Luke 16:18**, Jesus' words are recorded without the exception clause. *"Whoever divorces his wife and marries another commits adultery against her."*

Why the difference? Likely because Matthew was writing for a Jewish audience, where the rabbinic debate about *porneia* mattered. Mark and Luke, writing for Gentiles, emphasize the permanence of marriage without nuances. For them, the heart of Jesus' teaching was simple: divorce is not God's design.

THE MIRROR OF CHRIST AND THE CHURCH

To understand Jesus' passion, we must remember that marriage is not just about human companionship. It is a picture of Christ and His church (Eph. 5:32). Christ does not divorce His bride. He pursues her, sanctifies her, and presents her blameless. Divorce mars that reflection.

Think of a mirror designed to reflect the face of Christ's covenant love. When marriage breaks, the mirror cracks. The reflection is distorted. Jesus defends marriage so fiercely because it carries the glory of the gospel. Marriage, in the eyes of Jesus, is a sacred covenant that reflects the unconditional love and commitment between Christ and His church. Divorce disrupts this beautiful reflection and distorts the message of grace and redemption that marriage is meant to portray. By upholding the sanctity of marriage, Jesus is protecting the very essence of His gospel–a love that is steadfast, unwavering, and everlasting. The brokenness of divorce is a painful reminder of the brokenness of humanity and the desperate need for the healing power of Christ's love.

PASTORAL INSIGHT: NOT LEGAL LOOPHOLES BUT HEART TRANSFORMATION

For modern readers, the temptation is to reduce Jesus' teaching to a set of legal formulas: "Am I allowed to divorce in this case? What if my spouse does X or Y?" But Jesus was never offering a list of loopholes. He was calling us back to the heart of God. Jesus was urging his followers to strive for a deeper understanding of love and commitment in marriage, rooted in the unchanging nature of God's love for humanity. Instead of seeking ways to circumvent the difficulties of marriage through legal technicalities, Jesus emphasized the importance of heart transformation and aligning our relationships with the love and grace of God. By focusing on the essence of the gospel and the healing power of Christ's love, believers can find strength and guidance in navigating the complexities of marriage with faith and perseverance.

The real question is not, *"When can I get out?"* But, *"How can I reflect Christ's covenant love in my marriage?"* Where covenant is broken by sin, Jesus offers both truth and grace: truth to expose sin, grace to heal hearts.

ILLUSTRATION: THE WEDDING RING

A wedding ring is a simple circle of metal, unbroken and unending. It symbolizes permanence. Imagine a man who decides one day that he no longer loves his wife, and he cuts his wedding ring in half to symbolize his new "freedom." The metal may be cut, but the meaning is lost.

This is what Jesus is teaching. Divorce may cut the legal bond, but it cannot undo the covenant reality. Only the sin of the deepest betrayal (*porneia*) creates a legitimate breach. All other cutting is a desecration of the covenant symbol. Marriage is a sacred covenant that involves making a promise to God in front of witnesses. When we exchange wedding rings, we are entering into a lifelong commitment to love and honor our spouse, no matter what challenges may come our way. Just as cutting a wedding ring does not dissolve the marriage, divorce does not erase the sacred bond between two people. It is a reminder that love is not just a feeling but a choice we make every day to honor and cherish the person we have committed our lives to.

PROPHETIC WARNING FOR TODAY

Our modern culture looks more like the days of Hillel than Shammai. Divorce "for any cause" has returned–for incompatibility, unhappiness, or even boredom. Papers are signed, vows are broken, and children are left in the wreckage. The church must hear Jesus' words afresh: "From the beginning it was not so."

The prophetic call of Christ is to raise marriage back to its sacred place–not just as a personal relationship, but as a prophetic sign to the world of covenant love.

CONCLUSION: THE STANDARD OF THE KINGDOM

Jesus does not lower the bar; He raises it. He calls us back to Eden, back to covenant, back to the one-flesh union that no man may separate. Divorce, in His teaching, is a tragic concession, not a convenient option. Yet even here, grace shines. For those scarred by unfaithfulness, He offers hope. He extends forgiveness to those who are suffering from guilt. For those still in covenant, He offers strength to endure and overcome.

CHAPTER 5

Paul's Teaching on Divorce

Paul's Counsel on Separation and Reconciliation

When we open Paul's first letter to the Corinthians, we are not stepping into a calm, orderly church. Corinth was one of the most immoral cities of the ancient world–a melting pot of Roman law, Greek philosophy, and pagan idolatry. Divorce in Roman society was rampant. Unlike Jewish law, where men had to issue a certificate, Roman husbands and wives could dissolve their marriages almost casually. All it took was a declaration before witnesses, and a covenant was dissolved. Women, though often disadvantaged, had more legal rights in Rome than in Jewish culture, and some used those rights freely.

Into this climate, the Corinthian believers struggled. Many were married before they came to Christ, some to spouses who remained in paganism. Some were abandoned because of their newfound faith. Others wondered whether holiness meant they should leave their unbelieving spouse. And still others wrestled with passion, celibacy, and the desire for remarriage. Paul's pastoral heart is revealed in 1

Corinthians 7, where he gives careful, Spirit-inspired counsel that has guided the church for centuries.

FAITHFULNESS AMONG BELIEVERS

Paul begins by reaffirming Jesus' command concerning marriages between believers:

"To the married I give this charge (not I, but the Lord): the wife should not separate from her husband (but if she does, she should remain unmarried or else be reconciled to her husband), and the husband should not divorce his wife." (1 Cor. 7:10–11)

Paul reminds his readers that Jesus Himself had spoken on this matter. Between two believers, divorce is not permitted except for the cause Jesus gave–sexual immorality. But Paul adds a practical note: if separation does occur (and sometimes it must, for safety or sanity), the only two biblical options are to remain unmarried or to pursue reconciliation.

This standard protects the holiness of Christian marriage. The Spirit Himself is a witness to the covenant between two believers. To break it casually is to despise the work of God. Paul insists a covenant among believers is sacred, and nothing short of betrayal can dissolve it. Marriage is a sacred bond that should not be taken lightly, as it is a reflection of the covenant between believers and God. Paul emphasizes the importance of upholding the sanctity of marriage, even in difficult circumstances. By maintaining a commitment to reconciliation or remaining unmarried if separation occurs, believers can honor the work of God in their union. Ultimately, the Spirit Himself is present in the covenant of marriage, and breaking it without just cause is a betrayal of both the partner and God.

MIXED MARRIAGES: BELIEVER AND UNBELIEVER

Paul also addresses a situation Jesus never faced in His earthly ministry: believers married to unbelievers. Many in Corinth asked, "If my spouse does not believe in Christ, should I divorce them to keep myself pure?" Paul answers firmly: *"If any brother has a wife who is an unbeliever, and she consents to live with him, he should not divorce her. If any woman has a husband who is an unbeliever, and he consents to live with her, she should not divorce him. For the unbelieving husband is made holy because of his wife, and the unbelieving wife is made holy because of her husband."* (1 Cor. 7:12–14)

This teaching is remarkable. The presence of the believing spouse sanctifies the unbeliever rather than polluting the believer. The marriage is covered, the children are set apart, and the household becomes a place where the influence of Christ can spread. Paul does not mean that the unbeliever is automatically saved, but that the covenant is made holy by the faith of one partner.

Think of it this way: a believer is like an altar in the home. Their prayers, their faith, and their Spirit-filled presence sanctify the space. Even an unbelieving spouse and children benefit from the covenant covering of that altar. Divorce, therefore, is not the answer. Covenant faithfulness may yet win the unbeliever to Christ. By remaining steadfast in their faith and commitment to the marriage, the believer can continue to be a beacon of Christ's love and grace within the household. Through prayer, patience, and unwavering faith, the believer can create an environment where the unbelieving spouse and children may come to know and experience the transformative power of Christ. Divorce should not be seen as the solution, but rather, as an opportunity for redemption and reconciliation through the power of covenant faithfulness. Ultimately, the believer's dedication to their marriage may serve as a powerful testimony that leads the unbeliever to a personal relationship with Christ.

THE PAULINE PRIVILEGE: ABANDONMENT

Still, Paul is no idealist. He knows that sometimes an unbelieving spouse will not endure the marriage. Persecution, ridicule, or outright hostility may drive them away. In such cases, Paul offers what has come to be called the **Pauline Privilege**:

"But if the unbelieving partner separates, let it be so. In such cases the brother or sister is not enslaved. God has called you to peace." (1 Cor. 7:15)

Here Paul introduces a principle of release. If the unbelieving spouse abandons the marriage, the believer is "not enslaved." The Greek phrase *"ou dedoulōtai"* means not bound, not chained, not under servitude. In other words, the believer is free–free to live in peace, free to move forward, and, by implication, free to remarry.

This is not permission for casual divorce. It is recognition that a covenant cannot exist where one partner has already destroyed it through abandonment. God, Paul insists, has called His children not to bondage, but to peace.

FUNCTIONAL ABANDONMENT IN MODERN TIMES

Paul spoke of unbelievers abandoning the marriage. But what of today, when even professing believers may act as covenant breakers? Here the principle still applies. Many pastors and counselors recognize that **functional abandonment** can occur when a spouse:

Physically abandons the home. Emotionally withdraws and neglects their spouse. Refuses to work on the relationship or seek help. Engages in behavior that is damaging to the marriage. In these cases, the hurt and betrayal can be just as real as if the spouse had physically left. The pain of functional abandonment is not to be taken lightly, and it is important for those experiencing it to seek guidance and support in navigating the complexities of such a situation. Ultimately, the goal is still reconciliation and restoration, but sometimes that may not be possible, and in those cases, God's desire for His children to live in peace must be honored.

Refuses intimacy, partnership, or any marital duties without repentance. This type of emotional abandonment can be incredibly painful and damaging to the overall health of the marriage. Without repentance and a willingness to work on rebuilding trust and connection, the relationship may continue to suffer. Seeking counseling and guidance from a trusted therapist or spiritual leader can help navigate the difficult emotions and decisions that come with functional abandonment. Ultimately, it is important to prioritize one's own well-being and mental health in such situations, even if that means making the difficult decision to separate or divorce in order to find peace and healing.

Engages in persistent abuse—verbal, emotional, or physical. Engaging in persistent abuse, whether it be verbal, emotional, or physical, is a clear sign that the marriage is toxic and damaging. It is crucial for the victim to prioritize their safety and well-being above all else, even if it means ending the relationship. Seeking support from a therapist or counselor can provide guidance and assistance in navigating the complexities of leaving an abusive marriage and beginning the healing process. Remember, no one deserves to endure abuse in any form, and taking steps to protect oneself is essential for a happier and healthier future.

Neglects provision, leaving the family without support. Neglecting provision for the family is yet another form of abuse that can have serious consequences. It is important for the victim to recognize this behavior as unacceptable and seek help in order to secure a stable and safe future for themselves and their loved ones. By reaching out for assistance, they can begin to rebuild their lives and create a positive environment free from harm and neglect. Remember, everyone deserves to be in a nurturing and supportive relationship, and taking action to address abuse is the first step towards achieving that.

In such cases, though the person remains physically present, they have abandoned covenant in spirit. Just as Paul's principle set believers free from the chains of abandonment, so too today, wisdom must discern when a covenant has already been destroyed by ongoing violation.

PAUL'S PASTORAL BALANCE

Paul's genius in 1 Corinthians 7 is his balance. He does not reduce marriage to legalities, nor does he treat covenant casually. He is both uncompromising in truth and tender in grace.

He honors singleness as a gift, reminding the unmarried that their devotion can be wholly to the Lord.

He recognizes human weakness: *"It is better to marry than to burn with passion"* (v. 9).

He insists on faithfulness where possible, but he refuses to bind believers in situations of abuse or abandonment.

Paul's goal is not to create new chains but to lead God's people into holiness and peace. Paul's wisdom in addressing marriage and singleness in 1 Corinthians 7 is evident in his compassionate approach to complex relational dynamics. He acknowledges the reality of human desires and weaknesses, yet emphasizes the importance of honoring God in all circumstances. By advocating for faithfulness and respect within marriage while also recognizing the need for freedom from toxic situations, Paul demonstrates a balanced perspective that upholds the values of holiness and peace within the Christian community. His teachings continue to offer guidance and insight for believers navigating the complexities of relationships in the modern world.

CASE STUDY: THE DESERTED SPOUSE

Imagine a young wife in Corinth. She has come to Christ, but her pagan husband mocks her prayers, ridicules her faith, and finally abandons her. Without Paul's counsel, she might live condemned, chained to a covenant that no longer exists. But Paul's words free her: "You are not enslaved. God has called you to peace." With these words, the deserted spouse is reminded of her worth and dignity in the eyes of God. Knowing that she is not a victim of her husband's actions gives her the freedom to move forward with grace and forgiveness. Paul's teachings provide her with the strength and clarity needed to navigate the challenges of her situation and find peace in her newfound faith. His wisdom continues to resonate through the ages, offering hope and healing to all who seek guidance in times of turmoil.

Picture a modern believer whose spouse refuses intimacy, abuses them verbally, and neglects the children. Though they remain in the house, they have abandoned the covenant in spirit. Paul's principle applies: the believer is not called to bondage but to peace. By following Paul's teachings, this modern believer can find the courage to confront their spouse's behavior and seek help for themselves and their children. They can draw on the strength of their faith to make difficult decisions and ultimately find peace in knowing they deserve better treatment. Just as Paul's wisdom has provided guidance for generations before, it continues to offer solace and direction to those facing challenging circumstances in their relationships.

PROPHETIC INSIGHT: COVENANT AND PEACE

Notice Paul's conclusion: "God has called you to peace." Marriage was never meant to be a prison of fear or despair. It was meant to be a sanctuary of love and covenant. When it becomes instead a place of torment, God's heart is not to bind His children but to release them into peace.

This is not a license to run from hard work or minor conflict. It is a recognition that covenant is sacred, and when one party has already broken it beyond repair, the other is not condemned to chains.

PASTORAL APPLICATION

Paul's teaching challenges both pastors and believers today. It reminds us:

Marriage between two believers must be guarded fiercely. Separation should be rare; reconciliation should always be pursued. However, when abuse, infidelity, or irreparable harm has been done, God does not expect His children to remain in a toxic and damaging situation. Instead, He offers freedom and restoration to those who have been hurt beyond repair. As pastors, it is our duty to provide support, guidance, and a safe space for those who find themselves in difficult marital situations, always pointing them towards the healing and grace of God. Marriage is a sacred covenant, but it is not meant to be a prison for those who are suffering.

Believers married to unbelievers must not see their situation as defiled but as sanctified by their faith. Their presence is a witness; their prayers, an altar. We must remind those struggling in their marriages that they are not alone and that there is hope for a better future. By offering love, understanding, and prayer, we can help them navigate through the darkness and find a path towards healing and restoration. Let us stand alongside them, lifting them up in prayer and showing them the unconditional love and grace of God. Marriage may have its challenges, but with faith and perseverance, all things are possible.

Where abandonment occurs—whether physical or functional—the believer is not bound. God calls them to peace. Let us be a beacon of hope for those who are facing abandonment in their marriages, reminding them that God's plan for them is one of peace and restoration. By extending our love and support to them, we can help them see that they are not alone in their struggles and that there is a way forward. Through faith and perseverance, they can find the strength to overcome their challenges and build a stronger, more fulfilling marriage. God's love and grace are always present, guiding us towards a brighter future.

CLOSING REFLECTION

Paul's teaching in Corinth reminds us that the gospel does not create new chains; it breaks them. It does not cheapen covenant; it sanctifies it. It does not ignore human brokenness; it speaks peace into it. His pastoral wisdom is as relevant today as it was in the first century.

As we move forward, we must remember: Jesus gave us the vision, and Paul gave us the application. Together, they remind us that marriage is holy, covenant is sacred, and God's desire for His children is not bondage but peace. As we navigate the complexities of relationships and marriage in our modern world, let us hold onto the truths that Paul imparted to the Corinthians. Let us remember that the gospel is a message of freedom, redemption, and restoration. It is a light that guides us through the darkness, leading us towards a future filled with hope and joy. May we always strive to emulate the love and grace that Jesus and Paul exemplified, knowing that in doing so, we honor God and honor the sacred covenant of marriage.

PART II

WHEN COVENANT BREAKS

CHAPTER 6

Abuse, Neglect, and Covenant Violation

When the Covenant Is Broken: Addressing Abuse and Neglect in Marriage

Divorce is never God's first intention. Marriage was designed to be a covenant of love, safety, and joy. Yet there are times when a spouse may cry out, "I am not safe in my own home. I am not loved in my own covenant. The one who vowed to cherish me is destroying me. These are not rare stories. They are whispered in church hallways, revealed in counseling sessions, and hidden in the bruises and broken spirits of men and women alike.

In this chapter, we must face a painful but necessary question: **What about abuse and neglect?** While the Bible speaks clearly about adultery and abandonment, the cries of the oppressed in marriage cannot be ignored. If the covenant is meant to reflect Christ's love for His church, what happens when that covenant becomes a place of violence and betrayal?

"The Lord was witness between you and the wife of your youth, to whom you have been faithless, though she is your companion and your wife by covenant. Did He not make them one, with a portion of the Spirit in their union? ... For the man who does not love his wife but divorces her, says the Lord, the God of Israel, covers his garment with violence." (Mal. 2:14–16)

The language is startling: **violence.** God equates faithless treatment of a spouse with violence, treachery, and betrayal. Abuse, whether physical, verbal, emotional, or sexual, is more than a "marriage problem." It is a violation of covenant at its deepest level.

Marriage is meant to mirror Christ's love for His bride (Eph. 5:25–33). Abuse distorts that mirror. Instead of laying down one's life for a spouse, the abuser uses their power to crush, manipulate, or control. Such behavior is not just a sin against a spouse—it is treachery against God, who is the witness of the covenant. It is a perversion of the sacred bond that marriage is meant to be. God's heart breaks for those who are suffering in abusive relationships, and He calls us to stand against such evil and protect the vulnerable. As followers of Christ, we must not turn a blind eye to abuse within our midst but instead confront it with love, truth, and justice. Let us strive to create marriages and relationships that truly reflect the selfless love and grace of our Savior.

PHYSICAL ABUSE: VIOLENCE AGAINST ONE'S OWN FLESH

Paul teaches, *"He who loves his wife loves himself. For no one ever hated his own flesh, but nourishes and cherishes it."* (Eph. 5:28–29). To strike a spouse, therefore, is to strike one's own flesh. It is self-destruction and covenant violation.

Physical abuse destroys trust, safety, and intimacy. It turns the home–

meant to be a sanctuary–into a battlefield. When bruises replace embraces, covenant is already broken. It is essential for couples to remember that physical abuse is a violation of the sacred covenant of marriage. By harming one's spouse, one is ultimately harming oneself. The destruction caused by physical abuse extends far beyond just the physical wounds but also destroys the trust, safety, and intimacy within the relationship. Instead of a sanctuary, the home becomes a place of fear and pain. It is crucial for couples to seek help and healing in order to restore the love and grace that should be the foundation of their marriage.

TESTIMONY: THE SILENT SUFFERING OF A SHEPHERD

He was a good man and a faithful servant of God, known among his congregation for humility, patience, and prayer. Two years after his wedding, God blessed him and his wife with a beautiful baby girl. To many, they looked like the perfect family–proof that obedience brings blessing. But behind closed doors, the story was very different.

It began with small arguments that grew into shouting. Soon the shouting turned into physical violence. The same hands that once held him in affection became instruments of pain. On more than one occasion, she struck him with such force that she drew blood. He hid the bruises beneath his shirt and the cuts behind rehearsed explanations. How could a pastor, a man of God, admit that the one he loved had become his aggressor?

For years he endured in silence, convinced that if he prayed more, fasted longer, or loved harder, things would change. His greatest fear was not for his safety but for the name of the Lord and the opinion of the church. "What would people think if they knew?" he often whispered in tears.

One evening, when their daughter was ten, the violence erupted again. She saw her mother strike her father with something sharp. Terrified, she called the police. When officers arrived, the pastor tried to protect his wife, refusing to press charges, but the state intervened on its own. A restraining order was issued, and for the first time in years, the man of God was forced to face both freedom and shame.

Years have passed since that night, yet the scars remain—some on his skin, most in his soul. Even though they are legally apart, he still wonders if ending the relationship would make him appear unfaithful. The trauma of the abuse is now joined by the torment of guilt. His heart asks, "If I walk away, will I betray the call? Will they still see me as a shepherd—or as a failure?"

But heaven's answer is different. God never intended covenant to become a cage. The same Word that commands fidelity also commands peace. The Scripture says, "God has called us to peace" (1 Corinthians 7:15). Staying in a situation that destroys the soul does not honor God; it denies His image in us.

This pastor's story reminds us that abuse, in any form and against any person, violates the very covenant marriage was meant to protect. Silence may preserve appearances, but it kills the spirit. Truth and healing begin the moment light enters the hidden places.

LESSONS FROM HIS JOURNEY

1. **Abuse has no gender.** Both men and women can suffer in silence, and the church must make room for all who need help.
2. **Covenant never authorizes cruelty.** God's design for marriage is peace, not punishment.

3. **Silence empowers bondage.** Healing begins when truth is spoken, even if whispers turn into headlines.
4. **Spiritual leadership does not cancel human need.** Pastors are not immune to pain; they need safe spaces to heal.
5. **Grace provides a path of peace.** When an unbelieving or abusive spouse departs from covenant living, Scripture releases the believer from bondage.

PROPHETIC DECLARATION

May every man or woman hidden behind ministry titles, yet bleeding in silence, find courage to speak, wisdom to act, and grace to heal. May the church rise to defend the wounded without judgment. And may the peace of God–stronger than shame–guard every heart that dares to step into the light. May every pastor struggling in silence find the support and healing they need within their community. It is important for the church to provide a safe space for all individuals, regardless of their title, to seek help and find peace. Let us stand together in unity to protect and uplift those who are hurting, showing them the love and grace of God in their time of need.

God never calls His children to remain in danger. Safety is not secondary to covenant; it is part of covenant. When physical abuse occurs without repentance, the abuser has already abandoned their vow to love and protect. It is our duty as a church to intervene and offer support to those experiencing abuse, guiding them towards safety and healing. By standing together in unity, we can create a community where all individuals feel valued and protected. Let us continue to show love and grace to those in need, reflecting the compassion and care of God in all that we do.

VERBAL AND EMOTIONAL ABUSE: WOUNDS WITHOUT SCARS

Not all abuse leaves visible marks. Words, attitudes, and patterns of manipulation can leave scars that run deeper than bruises. Verbal and emotional abuse can slowly chip away at a person's self-worth and confidence, leaving them feeling isolated and powerless. The wounds inflicted by cruel words and emotional manipulation can be just as damaging as physical abuse, if not more so. It is important to recognize that abuse in any form is not acceptable in a healthy relationship, and seeking help and support is crucial in breaking free from the cycle of abuse.

Proverbs 12:18 warns, "The *words of the reckless pierce like swords, but the tongue of the wise brings healing."*

Colossians 3:19 commands husbands: *"Love your wives, and do not be harsh with them."*

Emotional abuse may include constant criticism, humiliation, isolation from friends and family, or controlling every decision. The victim begins to question their worth, their sanity, and even their right to exist. Such abuse may not be shouted from pulpits, but it echoes in countless Christian homes. It is important for individuals in abusive relationships to recognize the signs of emotional abuse and reach out for help. No one deserves to be treated in such a demeaning and controlling manner, regardless of their faith or beliefs. Seeking support from trusted friends, family members, or professionals can provide the necessary strength and guidance to break free from the cycle of abuse and work towards healing and empowerment. Remember, you are worthy of love, respect, and a happy, healthy relationship.

CASE STUDY: BETRAYAL FOR PROFIT

A pastor friend once told me about a woman whose husband, in pursuit of advancement, arranged for her to accompany his supervisors to "social meetings." Three separate times he left her vulnerable to their sexual advances–essentially trafficking his own wife for the hope of promotion. After the third ordeal, she refused ever to go again. In response, he sent her a letter of divorce.

What could she do? What would God do? And what would Paul advise?

Scripture answers through principle rather than case law.

The covenant has already been violated. Malachi 2:14 calls marriage "the covenant of your God," and verse 16 declares that God hates "the man who covers his garment with violence." To hand one's spouse over to abuse is to shatter that covenant in the most violent way.

Paul's word in 1 Corinthians 7:15 applies: "If the unbelieving departs, let him depart. A brother or sister is not under bondage in such cases; God has called us to peace." Here "departing" includes actions that abandon or destroy the essence of the marriage bond.

Christ's heart would never require someone to remain in a covenant that has become a contract of exploitation. His ministry set captives free, not keeping them bound to torment.

Pastoral wisdom therefore upholds both protection and peace: the abused party is free to separate, to heal, and–should restoration prove impossible–to rebuild life under grace.

LESSONS FROM HER STORY

1. **Exploitation is abandonment.** When a spouse uses the other's body for gain, the covenant is broken.
2. **Silence protects predators.** The church must name abuse for what it is.
3. **God's peace outranks social appearance.** Remaining in danger does not glorify God.
4. **Grace releases the victim, not the oppressor.** Mercy covers repentance, not manipulation.
5. **Healing begins with truth.** What is exposed can be redeemed.

PROPHETIC DECLARATION

May every hidden victim of betrayal find the courage to speak. May justice roll down like waters, and may the God who sees restore dignity, peace, and purpose to those whose trust was sold for profit. The covenant-keeping God still heals the violated and calls them to freedom.

May the power of truth and accountability break the chains of silence and bring light to the darkness of abuse. Let us stand in solidarity with the oppressed and work towards a society where the vulnerable are protected and the perpetrators are held accountable for their actions. May we all strive to create a world where love, justice, and healing prevail.

NEGLECT: THE SILENT ABANDONMENT

Neglect is another form of covenant violation. Scripture speaks directly to this in **Exodus 21:10–11**. A husband was commanded to provide his wife with food, clothing, and marital rights. If he failed, she was to go free. The principle is clear: neglect of basic marital responsibilities is a form of abandonment.

Paul reinforces this in **1 Timothy 5:8**: *"If anyone does not provide for his relatives, and especially for members of his household, he has denied the faith and is worse than an unbeliever."*

Neglect may not shout, but it whispers destruction into a marriage. A husband who refuses to work, a wife who refuses intimacy, and a partner who refuses emotional presence, all create a vacuum where covenant is starved to death.

TESTIMONY: THE COVENANT THAT REFUSED TO DIE

She stood before God and witnesses on September 24, 1966, at 10:00 a.m., radiant with expectation. My mother entered her marriage believing, as so many do, that love and faith would be enough to sustain it. But the journey that followed tested every vow she ever made.

My father was a man of charm and potential, yet his struggle with other women and his inability to stay anchored in covenant brought pain that few could endure. Soon after the wedding, he drifted away. He returned briefly to conceive me, left again, came back years later to conceive my sister Suzie, and then disappeared for good.

From that moment, my mother lived what I can only describe as a one-sided covenant. She remained married in name but alone in reality–raising her children single-handedly, fighting financial hardship, and waging unseen battles in prayer. Many nights she fought in the Spirit against the influences and women who surrounded my father's life, standing in the gap for a man who had long left her side.

She never saw herself as free to move on; she believed faithfulness meant staying until death, even if love had died decades before. Her endurance was heroic, yet it was also a portrait of what happens when revelation is missing.

Had she known the Word in its fullness–that "if the unbelieving departs, let him depart; a brother or sister is not under bondage in such cases" (1 Corinthians 7:15)–her story might have been written differently. Knowledge would have spared her years of silent suffering. Grace would have released her sooner.

Still, I honor her not for what she didn't know, but for the faith she lived with the light she had. She fought for a covenant she believed in, stood her ground in prayer, and proved that even in ignorance of the Word, God's mercy upholds the sincere.

When my father passed on September 11, 2012, she was still legally his wife–forty-six years after that wedding morning. Yet in heaven's eyes, she had already graduated with honor: a woman who loved beyond reason, forgave beyond measure, and endured beyond understanding.

Her story serves as a reminder that covenant faithfulness without revelation results in captivity, but faithfulness empowered by revelation results in freedom. God never asked His children to suffer in ignorance; He calls us to walk in truth, where grace and peace abound.

LESSONS FROM HER JOURNEY

6. **Ignorance of truth prolongs unnecessary pain.** What we do not know can keep us bound even when grace says we are

free.
7. **Endurance without revelation may preserve appearances but cost inner life.** God desires obedience informed by light, not suffering in darkness.
8. **Grace meets us where knowledge is lacking.** God still honors sincerity, even when understanding is incomplete.
9. **Scripture, not emotion, must be the source of covenant faithfulness.** Love without truth can lead to bondage, but truth with love leads to peace.
10. **Her life still speaks.** What she bore in silence has now become a testimony that sets others free.

PROPHETIC DECLARATION

May the God who redeemed her tears redeem the years of all who read this story. May revelation replace confusion, wisdom replace guilt, and grace rewrite the endings of those who have suffered without knowing they were already free. May this story serve as a beacon of hope for those who feel trapped in their own struggles, reminding them that God's love and truth are the keys to true liberation. Let us be inspired by her example of faithfulness, and may we also walk in covenant with God, guided by His Word and fueled by His love. And may we all experience the transformative power of God's redemption in our lives, turning our pain into purpose and our trials into triumphs.

GOD HAS CALLED US TO PEACE

Paul's words in **1 Corinthians 7:15** echo loudly here: *"God has called you to peace."* Marriage is not meant to be a cage of suffering. When abuse or neglect turns covenant into torment, the victim is not bound to remain enslaved.

This does not mean every difficult marriage is grounds for divorce. Conflict, imperfection, and hardship are part of life. However, persistent abuse, unrepentant neglect, and violent betrayal are not "marriage struggles." They are **covenant-breaking sins.**

TESTIMONY: LOVE THAT FOUND ITS WAY HOME AGAIN

Bertha married a man who served in the military–disciplined in uniform, yet undisciplined in the sacred vows of marriage. Though blessed with four beautiful children, their home slowly unraveled under the weight of his unfaithfulness. Each promise he made dissolved into another betrayal until finally he declared that marriage was too confining for the life he wanted. He divorced Bertha and walked away, certain that freedom waited beyond the boundaries of covenant.

Seventeen long years passed. The children became adults, built families of their own, and gave Bertha grandchildren who adored her. Yet even as generations grew, a quiet wound lingered–the absence of a father and grandfather who had chosen the road of self-will. Bertha, however, refused to let bitterness become her legacy. She worked hard, prayed fervently, and loved deeply, trusting God to be the husband of the forsaken and the defender of the faithful. Her strength became the anchor of the family.

Then one day, the unexpected happened. The same man who had once walked away came knocking again–this time not as a soldier looking for adventure, but as a broken man seeking mercy. Age and regret had taught him what youth and pride had blinded him to see: that the greatest freedom is found inside covenant love. He asked for forgiveness. The children, now parents themselves, struggled; decades of silence cannot be erased by a single apology. Yet Bertha, moved by grace, chose the higher road. "If God could forgive me," she said softly, "how could I not forgive him?"

I had the honor of officiating their remarriage in my office on a quiet Tuesday morning. There were no flowers or crowds, only two people standing once again before the God of covenant. When the ceremony ended, I told them, "This time, build the marriage you both always hoped for." We sent them away with a paid honeymoon for the rest of the week so they could begin anew, not as victims of the past but as witnesses of redemption.

That Sunday, I presented them to the church. When they walked in, hand in hand, the congregation rose to their feet. Tears flowed as children, grandchildren, and spiritual sons and daughters saw before them the undeniable evidence of God's restoring power. Their story needed no sermon; it preached grace louder than any words could.

LESSONS FROM THEIR JOURNEY

No distance is too great for grace to travel. Seventeen years and two generations later, mercy still found a way.

Forgiveness opens doors that time alone cannot. Only a heart surrendered to God can welcome the prodigal home.

Restoration heals more than two people–it heals families. Grandchildren inherit peace when parents choose grace.

True repentance redeems wasted years. What pride destroyed, humility rebuilt.

God delights in rewriting family stories. Covenant love, once broken, became a testimony that generations will tell.

PROPHETIC DECLARATION

May the same grace that brought Bertha and her husband back together also come into every home where there has been regret and separation. May mercy mend broken families and let children and grandchildren see love resurrected. The God who restored their covenant still rebuilds households today.

THE ROLE OF THE CHURCH: SHEPHERD OR SILENT PARTNER?

Too often, the church has erred in its counsel. Victims are told to endure. Abusers are shielded because of their public reputation. Divorce is condemned more loudly than the violence that caused it. In such cases, the church becomes complicit in covenant violation.

The church must instead:

Protect the vulnerable. Provide support and resources for those in abusive situations. Encourage accountability and repentance for those who have caused harm. Promote healing and restoration for families that have been broken. By actively working to uphold the sanctity of marriage while also prioritizing the safety and well-being of all individuals, the church can truly fulfill its role as a shepherd and not a silent partner in addressing issues of family dysfunction and violence.

Confront the abuser with both truth and discipline. It is crucial for the church to confront the abuser with both truth and discipline, holding them accountable for their actions and providing them with the opportunity for repentance and change. By doing so, the church can help break the cycle of abuse and prevent further harm from being inflicted. It is only through taking a stand against abuse and actively working towards promoting healing and restoration that the church can truly fulfill its duty to protect and support all members of its community.

Create safe spaces where victims can find refuge. The church can provide a place of comfort and support for those who have suffered abuse by creating safe spaces where victims can find refuge. It is essential for the church to prioritize the well-being and safety of its members, especially those who have experienced trauma. By providing a sanctuary for victims to seek help and healing, the church can demonstrate its commitment to justice and compassion for all who have suffered at the hands of abusers. In doing so, the church can truly embody its values of love, forgiveness, and redemption.

Preach that God hates violence as much as He hates divorce. It is crucial for the church to actively work towards preventing abuse and supporting those who have been affected by it. By speaking out against violence and offering a safe space for victims to seek help, the church can play a vital role in breaking the cycle of abuse and promoting healing within the community. Through education, advocacy, and compassion, the church can truly embody the message of love and justice that is at the core of its beliefs.

PROPHETIC WARNING

When churches protect abusers rather than victims, they desecrate the altar of covenant and grieve the Spirit of God. The church must also offer support and resources to those who have experienced abuse, guiding them towards healing and justice. By standing up for the oppressed and holding perpetrators accountable, the church can truly embody the love and justice of God. Failure to do so not only perpetuates harm but also tarnishes the reputation and integrity of the church as a whole. It is crucial for the church to prioritize the safety and well-being of all its members, living out the values of compassion, truth, and righteousness.

FORGIVENESS AND RESTORATION

What of forgiveness? Victims are often pressured to forgive and reconcile quickly. Yet forgiveness does not mean returning to danger. Forgiveness releases bitterness; reconciliation requires repentance and proven change. It is important for the church to prioritize the healing and safety of the victims first and foremost. Forgiveness should not be rushed or forced, as true reconciliation can only come when there is genuine remorse and a commitment to change from the perpetrator. By prioritizing the well-being of all members and holding perpetrators accountable, the church can truly embody the values of compassion, truth, and righteousness in a way that reflects the love and justice of God.

True restoration involves:

Confession of sin. Repentance. Making amends. Seeking forgiveness. These are all crucial steps in the process of true restoration within the church community. Without these essential components, reconciliation cannot be fully achieved. It is only through genuine humility and a willingness to change that healing and unity can be restored within the body of believers. May we always strive to uphold these principles in our pursuit of justice and grace.

Genuine repentance, accountability, and a genuine desire to make things right are all essential elements in the process of true restoration. It is through acknowledging our faults, seeking forgiveness, and taking concrete steps towards reconciliation that we can truly reflect the love and mercy of God in our relationships with one another. As we continue to practice humility and grace, may we always remember that true restoration is a journey that requires patience, understanding, and a commitment to seeking justice and righteousness in all that we do. Let us never waver in our pursuit of healing and unity within the church community, always striving to be vessels of God's love and forgiveness in all that we say and do.

Accountability structures are essential in ensuring that we remain accountable to one another and to God. By holding each other responsible for our actions and behaviors, we can foster a culture of transparency and trust within our community. Through open communication and a willingness to address conflicts and issues head-on, we can work towards building a stronger and more unified body of believers. Let us not shy away from the difficult conversations or the challenging moments, but instead lean into them with courage and a commitment to growth and reconciliation. Together, we can create a community that reflects the love and grace of our Savior, Jesus Christ.

A long process of rebuilding trust. This process may be difficult and require time and effort, but it is essential for healing and growth within our community. By facing our challenges with honesty and humility, we can move forward together towards a brighter future. Let us remember that through our shared faith and commitment to one another, we can overcome any obstacles and emerge stronger than before. Together, we can rebuild trust and create a community that shines with the light of God's love.

Where there is **no repentance, there can be no restoration**. The abused may forgive in their heart, but reconciliation is not demanded by God when safety and covenant are continually violated. It is crucial that those who have caused harm take responsibility for their actions and seek forgiveness with a genuine heart. Without true repentance, there can be no real healing or restoration in our community. It is important to prioritize the safety and well-being of all members, and those who have violated trust must be held accountable for their actions. Only through sincere repentance and a commitment to change can we truly rebuild trust and create a community that reflects God's love and grace.

PASTORAL APPLICATION

Abuse is not "marital difficulty"; it is covenant treachery. As pastors and spiritual leaders, it is our duty to address instances of abuse within our congregations with the seriousness and gravity they deserve. We must not minimize or dismiss abuse as simply a marital issue but rather acknowledge it for what it truly is: a betrayal of the sacred covenant between partners. It is essential that we provide support and resources for those who have been harmed while also holding the abuser accountable for their actions. By upholding the values of justice, compassion, and accountability, we can work towards creating a community that is safe, supportive, and reflective of God's love. For example, if a member of our congregation comes forward with allegations of domestic violence, we must respond swiftly and compassionately. This may involve connecting the victim with local shelters or counseling services while also encouraging the abuser to seek help through therapy or support groups. By taking a strong stance against abuse and providing resources for both victims and perpetrators, we can show that our community is committed to promoting healing and preventing future harm.

Neglect is not a minor weakness; it is abandonment in slow motion. We must be vigilant in our efforts to address and combat domestic violence within our congregation, as neglecting to take action only perpetuates the cycle of harm. It is our duty as members of the community to support and uplift those who are suffering and to hold those responsible for their actions, accountable. By actively promoting a culture of love, compassion, and accountability, we can create a safe and nurturing environment where all individuals can thrive and find healing. Let us stand together in solidarity against abuse, for it is only through unity and empathy that we can truly reflect the love of God in our actions. For example, our congregation could establish a support group for survivors of domestic violence, providing them with a safe space to share their experiences and receive guidance from trained professionals. Additionally, we could organize educational workshops and training sessions to raise awareness about the signs of abuse and empower individuals to intervene in potentially harmful situations.

Victims must be believed, protected, and healed. By coming together as a community, we can break the cycle of abuse and create a safer, more compassionate environment for all. It is our duty as believers to speak out against injustice and ensure that all individuals are treated with dignity and respect. Through our collective efforts, we can make a positive impact and show others the true power of love and support. Together, we can make a difference and bring hope to those who have experienced the trauma of abuse.

REFLECTION

Have we, as the church, sometimes treated victims of abuse as though their suffering was less important than preserving appearances?

Do we understand that peace, safety, and love are not optional in covenant, but essential?

How can we restore the prophetic witness of marriage when so many covenants are desecrated by hidden violence?

Prayer

Lord, You are a refuge for the oppressed and a stronghold in times of trouble. We cry out for every man or woman living in fear behind closed doors. Shine your light into hidden places. Expose the works of darkness. Heal the wounded, confront the abuser, and restore covenant where true repentance flows. Where peace is absent, call Your children into freedom. In Jesus' name, amen.

THE SHATTERED HOME: THE IMPACT OF DIVORCE ON CHILDREN, COMMUNITY, AND NATIONS

Echoes Beyond the Home

DIVORCE IS NEVER AN ISOLATED event. It is not only the unraveling of two lives but also the tearing apart of a covenant that reverberates outward like ripples on a pond. What begins in the home spreads to children, extended families, communities, and even the destiny of nations. When God declared in Malachi 2:16, *"I hate divorce,"* it was not because He hates people who divorce, but because He sees how deeply it wounds generations and destabilizes the very fabric of society. The impact of divorce on children is especially profound, as they are often caught in the middle of the conflict and forced to navigate the emotional turmoil that comes with it. Extended families are also affected, as relationships become strained and loyalties are divided. Communities feel the ripple effect as well, with an increase in single-parent households and a shift in social norms. Family units are the foundation of society, so the instability that divorce causes can ultimately have a significant impact on the future of nations. It is a sobering reminder of the importance of preserving and protecting the sanctity of marriage.

THE IMPACT ON CHILDREN: SILENT CASUALTIES OF BROKEN COVENANTS

Children are often the hidden victims of divorce. Parents may experience relief after years of conflict, but children rarely see separation as liberation. For them, it is often confusion, fear, and a lifelong struggle with questions of identity and belonging. They may blame themselves for their parents' separation, leading to feelings of guilt and low self-worth. The absence of a stable family unit can also affect their emotional and psychological development, impacting their relationships and ability to trust others in the future. As a society, it is crucial to provide support and resources for children going through divorce to help them navigate these challenging times and build resilience for the future.

BIBLICAL INSIGHT:

Malachi 2:15 reminds us that God makes husband and wife one because He desires "godly offspring." Divorce disrupts this divine purpose. It fragments the spiritual covering that children were meant to grow under.

PSYCHOLOGICAL AND SOCIOLOGICAL FINDINGS

Studies show that children of divorce are more likely to suffer from anxiety, depression, academic struggles, and behavioral issues. This highlights the importance of providing children of divorce with the necessary tools and support to help them cope with the emotional and psychological effects of their parents' separation. By offering resources such as counseling, support groups, and access to mental health professionals, we can help children develop the resilience needed to overcome these challenges and thrive in the face of adversity. It is our responsibility as a society to ensure that children of divorce are given the opportunity to heal and grow into healthy, well-adjusted individuals despite the difficulties they may face.

They are statistically more prone to engage in risky behaviors as teens and to experience broken relationships in adulthood. By addressing these issues early on and providing children with the necessary tools and support, we can help mitigate the long-term effects of divorce on their emotional and psychological well-being. It is crucial for parents to put aside their differences and focus on co-parenting effectively to ensure their child's stability and happiness. With the right resources and guidance, children can learn to cope with the changes brought on by divorce and grow into resilient and successful individuals.

Many develop a fear of commitment, repeating the cycle of instability they witnessed in their own homes. However, with the proper intervention and therapy, children can work through their fears and insecurities to form healthy relationships in the future. It is important for parents to seek out professional help for their children if needed and to create a supportive and nurturing environment for them to heal and thrive. By breaking the cycle of instability and providing children with the tools they need to navigate the challenges of divorce, we can help them build a strong foundation for their future happiness and success.

CASE STUDY

James was twelve when his parents divorced. He remembers hearing the fights, but he also remembers clinging to the hope that one day they would make up. When his father finally left, James didn't just lose a parent at home; he lost his sense of security in the world. As a man, he found it difficult to trust women, always expecting abandonment. His father's departure had planted a seed of fear that bore fruit decades later.

This fear manifested in his relationships, causing him to push people away before they could hurt him. He struggled with feelings of inadequacy and unworthiness, believing that he was not deserving of love or happiness. Therapy helped James unpack these deep-seated beliefs and heal from the wounds of his parents' divorce. Through counseling, he learned to trust again, to communicate openly and honestly with his partners, and to let go of the fear that had held him captive for so long. James was able to create healthy, fulfilling relationships and break the cycle of pain and dysfunction that had plagued his family for generations.

SPIRITUAL CONSEQUENCE

Children of divorce often wrestle with their image of God as Father. If earthly fathers abandon, how can a heavenly Father be trusted? Unless the church steps in with intentional healing and discipleship, these wounds may calcify into unbelief.

THE IMPACT ON FAMILIES: RIPPLES THROUGH GENERATIONS

Divorce doesn't just break two people apart; it ripples through extended families. Children of divorce often carry the burden of brokenness into their own relationships and families, perpetuating the cycle of dysfunction. Siblings may struggle with their own feelings of abandonment and fear of commitment, leading to strained relationships with their partners and children. The impact of divorce can be felt for generations, unless intentional healing and restoration take place within the family unit. It is crucial for the church and community to offer support and guidance to those affected by divorce in order to break the cycle of pain and dysfunction for future generations.

Grandparents lose consistent contact with grandchildren. This loss can be devastating for both the grandparents and the grandchildren, as they miss out on the opportunity to form close relationships and create lasting memories together. Grandparents may also feel a sense of helplessness as they watch their own children struggle with the aftermath of divorce. It is important for the church and community to provide resources and assistance to grandparents who are navigating this difficult situation, as their support can help mitigate some of the negative effects of divorce on future generations.

Siblings are forced into divided loyalties, sometimes aligning with one parent over another. This can create tension and conflict within the family, as siblings may feel pressured to choose sides or feel guilty for maintaining relationships with both parents. It is crucial for parents to prioritize the well-being of their children and work together to co-parent effectively, ensuring that their children are not caught in the middle. By fostering open communication and cooperation, families can help their children navigate the challenges of divorce and maintain strong relationships with all family members. It is important for everyone involved to prioritize the needs of the children and work towards creating a supportive and loving environment for them to thrive in.

Holidays become battlegrounds of scheduling instead of celebrations of unity. It is essential for parents to set aside their differences and focus on what is best for their children during and after a divorce. By putting their children's needs first, parents can create a stable and nurturing environment that allows their children to feel secure and loved. Through effective co-parenting and communication, families can ensure that holidays are not overshadowed by conflict but instead are filled with joy and cherished memories for all family members. It is crucial for parents to work together to create a peaceful and harmonious co-parenting relationship that prioritizes the well-being and happiness of their children.

ILLUSTRATION

Imagine a family gathering for Christmas. In a home where covenant remains intact, the day is filled with laughter, shared meals, and the joy of generations united. But in the aftermath of divorce, Christmas becomes two gatherings, then three, each with its own undercurrent of tension. Instead of one family altar, multiple fractured altars emerge. The children are caught in the middle, feeling torn between their parents and struggling to navigate the complexities of divided loyalties. The once unified family dynamic is now strained, with the holidays serving as a painful reminder of what once was. However, with open communication, compromise, and a shared commitment to putting the children first, co-parents can work towards creating new traditions and memories that prioritize the well-being and happiness of their children, even in the face of divorce.

PROPHETIC INSIGHT

Divorce multiplies altars. Instead of one covenantal place where God's presence is honored, fractured homes scatter affections and loyalties. This is not just relational—it is spiritual. Broken altars produce broken sacrifices.

THE IMPACT ON COMMUNITIES: BROKEN HOMES, BROKEN STREETS

Strong families are the backbone of strong communities. When homes are stable, children thrive, crime diminishes, and social trust increases. When homes collapse, the effects spill into schools, neighborhoods, and local economies. Communities with high rates of divorce often experience higher levels of crime, poverty, and social unrest. Children from broken homes are more likely to struggle academically and emotionally, leading to increased need for social services and intervention. The ripple effect of divorce can be felt throughout a community, impacting everything from property values to community cohesion. It is clear that the health of our families directly impacts the health of our neighborhoods and cities.

BIBLICAL REFLECTION

Psalm 127:1 declares, *"Unless the Lord builds the house, those who build it labor in vain."* Families are not only private units but also spiritual foundations for entire societies. When they crumble, the walls of the community are weakened.

SOCIOLOGICAL OBSERVATIONS

Communities with high divorce rates often see higher poverty levels. This is because divorce can lead to financial instability for families, which in turn can impact the overall economic health of a community. Additionally, children from divorced families may struggle academically and socially, which can have long-term consequences for the community as a whole. It is clear that supporting strong, healthy families is essential for the well-being of our communities.

Schools face increased behavioral issues as children carry trauma into classrooms. This can lead to lower academic performance and higher dropout rates, further perpetuating the cycle of poverty and instability. Teachers may also struggle to provide the necessary support and resources for students dealing with the emotional aftermath of divorce. In order to address these challenges, it is important for schools to provide counseling services and create a supportive environment for children from divorced families. By investing in the well-being of these students, communities can help break the cycle of poverty and ensure a brighter future for all.

Social service systems are overwhelmed, diverting resources that could have built community prosperity. By prioritizing the mental health and emotional needs of children from divorced families, schools can help prevent long-term negative effects on their academic performance and overall well-being. Additionally, by providing counseling services and a supportive environment, schools can empower these students to overcome the challenges they face and thrive in their educational pursuits. Ultimately, investing in the success of children from divorced families will not only benefit the individuals themselves but also contribute to the overall prosperity and stability of the community as a whole.

CASE STUDY

In one American city, sociologists tracked neighborhoods with high family breakdown. These areas consistently had higher gang activity, lower graduation rates, and more violent crime. The conclusion was clear: where fathers were absent and marriages broken, the community itself suffered instability.

This instability manifested in various ways, from economic struggles to social unrest. Children growing up in these neighborhoods faced increased obstacles in achieving academic success and often lacked the necessary support systems to thrive. As a result, many of them were more susceptible to negative influences and engaged in risky behaviors, further perpetuating the cycle of poverty and crime. The impact of family breakdown on the community is undeniable, highlighting the need for interventions and support systems to address the root causes of these issues. By investing in programs that provide resources and guidance to children from divorced families, we can help break this cycle and create a more stable and prosperous community for all its residents.

PASTORAL REFLECTION

When pastors spend more time counseling fractured families than equipping stable ones, the church's mission slows. Community evangelism becomes crisis management. Instead of sending families out as lights, the church spends its energy patching wounds.

This shift in focus can have detrimental effects on the overall health and growth of the church community. It is crucial for pastors to not only provide support and guidance to families in crisis but also to invest in programs that promote healthy relationships and prevent issues from escalating to the point of breakdown. By prioritizing the equipping of stable families, the church can create a foundation of strength and resilience that will benefit the entire community in the long run. This proactive approach can help break the cycle of dysfunction and create a more vibrant and thriving church community.

THE IMPACT ON NATIONS: FOUNDATIONS SHAKEN

A nation is only as strong as its families. This is not mere rhetoric but biblical reality.

Psalm 11:3 asks, "If *the foundations are destroyed, what can the righteous do?*" Family is the foundation of civilization. Governments, economies, and cultures are built on the stability of the home. When family covenants collapse, the national foundation weakens.

HISTORICAL NOTE

The Roman Empire, at its height, saw marriage and family collapse. Divorce became commonplace. Children were abandoned. Sexual immorality was rampant. Historians often note that the breakdown of the family was one of the precursors to Rome's decline.

The consequences of a weakened family structure are evident throughout history, as seen in the decline of the Roman Empire. Without strong family foundations, societies struggle to maintain stability and cohesion. The breakdown of the family unit can lead to a myriad of social issues, including poverty, crime, and mental health problems. It is crucial for individuals and communities to prioritize the well-being of families in order to ensure a thriving and prosperous society. By upholding the values of commitment, love, and support within the family unit, we can create a solid foundation for future generations to build upon.

APPLICATION TO HAITI AND BEYOND

In Haiti, where I carry a deep burden, the effects of broken families are visible everywhere. Fatherlessness, poverty, and gang violence are not just political problems; they are the bitter fruit of broken homes. If we are to rebuild nations, we must begin by rebuilding families. Schools, governments, and economies cannot thrive where covenant is ignored.

The key to transforming Haiti and other nations in crisis lies in restoring the family unit. By promoting strong relationships between parents and children, we can break the cycle of dysfunction and poverty that plagues so many communities. It is through the power of love and commitment that we can create a brighter future for all. Let us work together to strengthen families and build a better world for generations to come.

PROPHETIC PARALLEL

Divorce in the home mirrors division in the nation. Just as a husband and wife in strife weaken their household, political leaders in strife weaken their country. Healing at the family altar is therefore not only personal restoration but also national intercession. By fostering healthy and loving relationships within our families, we are not only creating a strong foundation for future generations but also contributing to the overall well-being of our society. Just as a broken family can lead to dysfunction and poverty, a divided nation can lead to chaos and instability. Let us strive to mend the fractures in our families and communities so that we may pave the way for a more harmonious and prosperous future for all.

DIVORCE AS SPIRITUAL WARFARE

Behind the social and emotional consequences lies a deeper reality: divorce is spiritual warfare. Satan hates marriage because it reflects Christ and the church (Eph. 5:32). If he can shatter the home, he can distort the gospel message and cripple future generations. By recognizing divorce as a tool of the enemy, we can approach the issue with a renewed sense of urgency and determination. It is essential for us to fight against the forces seeking to destroy the sacred institution of marriage and protect the family unit at all costs. Through prayer, perseverance, and a commitment to upholding biblical values, we can combat the spiritual warfare surrounding divorce and work towards healing and restoration in our families and communities.

Divorce robs children of a godly heritage. It is our responsibility as believers to stand firm in our faith and resist the temptation to give in to the lies of the enemy. We must model healthy, loving marriages for our children and grandchildren, showing them the true beauty and sanctity of the marital covenant. By staying rooted in God's word and seeking His guidance in all things, we can break the cycle of divorce and create a legacy of strength and unity for generations to come. Let us join together in prayer and unity, fighting against the forces of darkness that seek to tear apart what God has joined together. However, there are instances where even devout believers who stand firm in their faith still end up in divorce due to various reasons such as infidelity, abuse, or irreconcilable differences. It is important to acknowledge that not all marriages can be saved simply by staying rooted in God's word, and sometimes divorce may be the best solution for both parties to find peace and healing.

Divorce erodes the prophetic witness of Christian families. Marriages are meant to reflect the love and unity of Christ and the Church, and divorce can be a painful and difficult decision. However, it is essential to remember that God is a God of grace and forgiveness, and He can bring healing and restoration even in the midst of brokenness. As Christian communities, we must offer support and understanding to those going through divorce, showing them love and compassion rather than judgment and condemnation. By coming together in prayer and unity, we can be a source of strength and hope for those facing the challenges of divorce, helping them to find healing and wholeness in God's love.

Divorce destabilizes nations by destabilizing their smallest units. Divorce not only affects individuals and families, but it can also have wider societal implications. When marriages dissolve, it can lead to a breakdown of the family unit, which is the foundation of society. This can have a ripple effect, causing instability and unrest within communities and ultimately impacting the stability of the nation as a whole. It is therefore crucial for us as a society to support and uplift those going through divorce, helping them to navigate this difficult time with grace and compassion. Through our collective efforts, we can work towards building stronger, more resilient communities that are able to weather the storms of life.

This is why the enemy invests so much energy in destroying marriages. Every broken home is not only a personal tragedy but also a spiritual victory for the forces of darkness. It is important for us to recognize the importance of strong and healthy relationships in our society. By supporting those going through divorce and helping them heal, we are not only aiding individuals in their time of need but also contributing to the overall well-being of our communities. We must stand together and fight against the destructive forces that seek to tear us apart and instead strive towards building a society that values and nurtures relationships for the benefit of all. Let us be a beacon of hope and compassion in a world that often feels dark and turbulent, shining light on the path towards healing and unity.

THE CHURCH'S PROPHETIC RESPONSIBILITY

The church cannot stand idly by while divorce ravages families, children, and nations. We must:

Preach the sanctity of covenant boldly. We must remind our congregations of the importance of commitment and fidelity in marriage, encouraging couples to seek counseling and support when facing challenges. Additionally, we must advocate for policies and programs that support healthy relationships and provide resources for those in need. As a church, it is our duty to be a voice of truth and love in a world that often glorifies individualism and instant gratification. Let us lead by example and show the world the transformative power of faith and community in building strong, thriving relationships.

Surround children of divorce with spiritual fathers and mothers who can provide guidance and support as they navigate the challenges of growing up in a broken home. By investing in the next generation and creating a network of loving and committed role models, we can help break the cycle of broken relationships and build a foundation of stability and love for future generations. Together, we can create a community where marriage is honored, families are supported, and individuals are encouraged to live out their faith in every aspect of their lives.

Let us not turn a blind eye to those struggling in their marriages, but instead offer a helping hand and a listening ear. By coming together as a community, we can provide the guidance and support needed to nurture and strengthen relationships. Let us be beacons of hope and love, showing others the beauty and fulfillment that comes from honoring our commitments and staying faithful to our partners.

Together, we can make a difference in the lives of those around us and create a world where healthy, loving relationships thrive.

Minister healing to families, not just individuals. By extending compassion and understanding to those experiencing difficulties in their marriages, we can help mend broken relationships and restore harmony within families. It is important to recognize that the well-being of a family unit is interconnected, and by ministering healing to families as a whole, we can create a ripple effect of positivity and growth. Let us not underestimate the power of our support in fostering strong, loving bonds that withstand the test of time and adversity. Together, we can be a source of strength and encouragement for those in need, ultimately building a community where healthy, thriving relationships are the norm.

Proclaim that rebuilding families is part of rebuilding nations. As believers, we must actively work towards restoring broken relationships and promoting strong family units. The church has a prophetic responsibility to address the issues of divorce and its impact on society. By preaching the sanctity of covenant, providing support to children of divorce, and ministering healing to families, we can play a crucial role in rebuilding nations from the ground up. Let us embrace this responsibility with courage and conviction, knowing that our efforts will bring about positive change in our communities and beyond.

ILLUSTRATION

In Nehemiah's day, when the walls of Jerusalem lay in ruins, each family was assigned a portion of the wall to rebuild. In the same way, the church can take on the task of rebuilding the broken walls of families and society by addressing the issue of divorce head-on. Just as each family in Nehemiah's time played a crucial role in rebuilding the city, so too can each member of the church play a vital role in restoring the fabric of society through their support and commitment to strengthening family units. Let us stand together in unity and purpose, knowing that our efforts will not be in vain but will lead to a brighter future for generations to come. Likewise, today each family in the church must be strengthened, so that together we rebuild the spiritual walls of our communities and nations.

CLOSING REFLECTION

Divorce is **more** than a personal failure. It is a spiritual and societal earthquake. Its aftershocks ripple through children, fracture families, destabilize communities, and weaken nations. Yet God's heart is always redemptive. He calls the church to be a place of healing for the broken, a sanctuary for children, a fortress for families, and an altar for nations.

As we come together as a church family, we have the opportunity to be agents of change and restoration in our communities and nations. Through our collective efforts and unity, we can make a lasting impact that will transcend generations. Let's work to mend the wounds left by divorce, strengthen families, and rebuild our communities while following God's redemptive heart. Together, we can be a beacon of hope and light in a world that is often dark and broken.

If we heal the family, we heal the nation. If we restore the covenant, we restore the altar. Let us not be complacent or apathetic, but rather proactive and intentional in our mission to bring about positive change. By showing love, grace, and compassion to those in need, we can create a ripple effect that spreads far and wide. Let us stand firm in our faith and trust that God will use us as instruments of His peace and reconciliation. Together, we can make a difference and leave a legacy of love and restoration for future generations to come.

CHAPTER 8

Family Altars and Generational Curses in Marriage

Heritage and Bondage

MARRIAGE DOES NOT EXIST IN a vacuum. Every couple brings into their union not only their personal experiences but also the **spiritual inheritance of their family line.** In Scripture, these inherited patterns are often tied to *altars*—places of covenant, worship, and sacrifice that either align with God or with darkness. Unless these family altars are dealt with, they continue to influence marriages and relationships, often without awareness. By recognizing and breaking generational curses associated with family altars, couples can create a new legacy of love and restoration for their own children and future generations. It is important for couples to identify any negative patterns or influences from their family backgrounds and address them through prayer, counseling, and intentional actions. By doing so, they can build a strong foundation for their marriage that is rooted in God's love and grace, rather than the darkness of the past.

WHAT ARE FAMILY ALTARS?

An altar in the Bible is more than a pile of stones. It is a **spiritual gateway**–a place where heaven and earth meet, where covenants are established, and where sacrifices invite either God's blessing or demonic influence.

Godly altars (like Abraham's in Genesis 12:7–8) establish covenant with the Lord and bring blessing to generations. Creating a family altar is a way for couples to invite God's presence into their marriage and home. By dedicating a specific space for prayer, worship, and reflection, they are actively building a spiritual foundation that will guide their relationship. Just as Abraham's altar brought blessings to his descendants, a family altar can serve as a reminder of God's faithfulness and grace for generations to come. It is a powerful symbol of commitment to each other and to God, setting the tone for a marriage that is firmly rooted in faith.

Ungodly altars (like those of Ahab and Jezebel in 1 Kings 16:32–33) invite bondage, idolatry, and curses that affect families for generations. Setting up a family altar may not necessarily guarantee a successful marriage or spiritual foundation, as relationships are complex and require more than just a physical symbol of commitment to thrive. Additionally, the presence of a family altar does not automatically protect against negative influences or guarantee blessings, as seen in the case of Ahab and Jezebel in the Bible. Therefore, it is crucial for couples to establish a family altar that is centered on God and His principles. This sacred space can serve as a place of unity, peace, and spiritual growth for the entire family. By intentionally creating a space for prayer and worship, couples are inviting God's presence and blessings into their marriage and home. In doing so, they are laying a strong foundation that will withstand the trials and challenges that come their way, ultimately leading to a relationship that is deeply rooted in faith and love.

A *family altar* can be literal (idolatrous practices, witchcraft, ancestral worship) or figurative (patterns of sin, addictions, abuse, betrayal). These altars cry out through the bloodline until someone confronts them in Christ. While creating a space for prayer and worship can be beneficial for spiritual growth, it is important to be cautious of potentially harmful practices or beliefs that may be associated with certain types of altars, whether literal or figurative. It is essential to discern and address any negative influences that could hinder true spiritual growth within the family.

BIBLICAL BASIS FOR GENERATIONAL IMPACT

Exodus 20:5–"I, *the LORD your God, am a jealous God, visiting the iniquity of the fathers on the children to the third and the fourth generation of those who hate me.*"

Lamentations 5:7 – "Fathers *sinned and are no more; it is we who have borne their iniquities.*"

John 9:2–3–The disciples ask if a man was born blind because of his parents' sin. Jesus shifts the perspective: not every suffering is generational, but some indeed flow from ancestral lines.

These verses show that sin can create patterns, passed down like spiritual DNA, until they are broken in Christ.

HOW FAMILY ALTARS AFFECT MARRIAGE

By laying a foundation of faith and values that can help couples overcome obstacles and strengthen their relationship, family altars create a space for prayer, reflection, and spiritual growth, allowing couples to connect on a deeper level and support each other in their journey together. By prioritizing their relationship with God and each other through regular devotion and communication at the family altar, couples can build a strong and lasting marriage that is rooted in love, trust, and mutual respect. While family altars can certainly provide a space for spiritual growth and connection, it is not necessarily a guarantee that couples will have a strong and lasting marriage solely based on this practice. Building a successful marriage requires more than just regular devotion and communication at the family altar, as external factors and individual differences also play a significant role in the success of a relationship.

PATTERNS OF INFIDELITY AND DIVORCE

If adultery or abandonment is common in a family line, children often repeat it unknowingly.

Example: Abraham lied about Sarah, Isaac repeated the same with Rebekah, and Jacob deceived for a blessing–patterns run through bloodlines. It is important for couples to be aware of these patterns and actively work to break the cycle through open communication and seeking the Holy Spirit for guidance. This awareness can help couples recognize destructive behaviors and work together to build a healthier relationship. By acknowledging the patterns of infidelity and divorce in their family history, couples can take proactive steps to prevent repeating them in their own marriage. Through prayer, open communication, and seeking guidance from the Holy Spirit couples can break free from negative generational cycles and create a strong and lasting bond. Recognizing the influence of family history on behavior can help couples navigate potential pitfalls and make conscious decisions to strengthen their marriage. While family altar practices can provide a strong foundation, addressing underlying issues and actively working towards a healthy relationship is essential for a successful and lasting marriage.

CYCLES OF ABUSE AND VIOLENCE

Where fathers were violent or mothers manipulative, children often carry the same spirit into their marriages. This perpetuates a cycle of abuse and violence that can be difficult to break. However, by acknowledging these patterns and actively working to address and change them, couples can create a new legacy for future generations. It is important for couples to seek therapy or counseling to address any unresolved trauma or negative influences from their family history in order to build a healthy and thriving marriage. Breaking free from these destructive cycles requires effort and dedication, but the rewards of a loving and harmonious relationship are well worth it.

This is not just "learned behavior"—it is the cry of an altar. By breaking free from the destructive cycles of abuse and violence, couples can create a new foundation for their relationship based on love, respect, and understanding. Seeking therapy or counseling can provide couples with the tools and support they need to address their past traumas and build a healthier future together. It is important to remember that change is possible and that by taking the necessary steps, couples can break free from the patterns that have been passed down through generations. The cry of an altar signifies a new beginning, a commitment to breaking free from the past and creating a brighter future for themselves and for their children.

By acknowledging the need for change and actively working towards it, couples can pave the way for a more fulfilling and harmonious relationship. Embracing this new chapter together can lead to a deeper connection and a stronger bond that will withstand any challenges that may come their way. In Psalm 51:10 – "Create in me a clean heart, O God, and renew a steadfast spirit within me" we are reminded that we have the power to start anew and make positive changes in our lives. Just as couples can come together at an altar to signify a new beginning, we too can make the choice to break free from negative patterns and create a brighter future for ourselves. By seeking God's guidance and actively working towards change, we can pave the way for a more fulfilling and harmonious life.

THE BLOODLINE

I once counseled a young couple who had every reason to succeed; educated, godly and in love. However, their marriage was characterized by constant suspicion and uncontrollable outbursts. As we prayed, the Spirit revealed that in both families, divorce was the norm: her grandparents, parents, and even uncles had divorced; his father had abandoned the family when he was a child. They were not just fighting each other, they were fighting family altars of broken covenant. Breaking free from generational patterns and curses requires intentional effort and a strong reliance on God's grace. By acknowledging the destructive cycles and actively seeking healing and restoration, this couple was able to break free from the bondage of their family history and create a new legacy of love and commitment. Through prayer, counseling, and a deep commitment to each other, they were able to overcome the odds and build a solid foundation for a lasting and healthy marriage.

Once they identified and renounced these altars in prayer, things shifted. They broke agreement with generational curses and dedicated their marriage as a godly altar unto the Lord. That day marked the beginning of healing.

As they continued to walk in faith and obedience, they saw God's hand at work in their relationship in ways they never thought possible. The wounds of the past began to heal, and they experienced a renewed sense of love, trust, and unity. Their marriage became a testimony of God's faithfulness and grace, inspiring others to seek healing and restoration in their own relationships. With each passing day, they grew stronger together, their bond deepening as they leaned on God for guidance and strength. The legacy of brokenness and pain was replaced with one of redemption and hope, a testament to the power of God to transform even the most broken of relationships.

HOW TO IDENTIFY FAMILY ALTARS

Look for patterns in the family line (divorce, addiction, abuse, barrenness, poverty). These patterns can often indicate the need for healing and restoration within the family, pointing to areas where a family altar may be necessary. By recognizing these patterns, individuals can begin to break the cycle of dysfunction and create a new legacy of love and unity. Establishing a family altar can help to bring about healing, reconciliation, and transformation, allowing God's faithfulness and grace to work in powerful ways within the family unit. By identifying these patterns and taking steps to establish a family altar, individuals can pave the way for a future filled with redemption and hope, breaking free from the legacy of brokenness and pain.

Notice **recurring crises** (marriages failing at the same stage, repeated miscarriages, infidelity). By acknowledging and addressing these recurring crises within the family, individuals can begin to understand the root causes and work towards healing and restoration. Establishing a family altar provides a sacred space for reflection, prayer, and seeking guidance from God to overcome these challenges. With a renewed focus on faith and unity, families can break free from the cycle of dysfunction and build a future filled with love, healing, and hope.

Pay attention to **words spoken** (family sayings like "In our family men always leave" or "No marriage in this house lasts"). Recognizing and challenging these negative family sayings can also help to shift the mindset and beliefs that have been ingrained over generations. By replacing these harmful narratives with positive affirmations and declarations of love and commitment, families can begin to create a new legacy of lasting relationships and strong bonds. It is important for individuals to seek counseling or therapy if needed in order to address any deep-seated issues that may be contributing to the dysfunction within the family. Through open communication, forgiveness, and a willingness to change, families can break free from destructive patterns and create a future filled with joy and peace.

Altars are revealed through **repetition**. What happens once may be chance; what happens generationally is covenant. By consistently practicing positive affirmations and declarations of love within the family, individuals can solidify their commitment to each other and create a strong foundation for future generations. Seeking counseling or therapy can help address underlying issues that may be causing dysfunction within the family, allowing for healing and growth to take place. As families work together to communicate openly, forgive past hurts, and make necessary changes, they can break free from destructive patterns and create a legacy of love, joy, and peace that will last for generations to come. Ultimately, the true power of family lies in the covenant of love and commitment that is passed down through the generations, creating a lasting bond that withstands the test of time.

BREAKING FAMILY ALTARS IN CHRIST

The good news is that the cross is stronger than any altar.

When families choose to break free from negative patterns and destructive influences, they can turn to the love and grace of Christ to guide them towards healing and restoration. By surrendering their brokenness to the power of the cross, families can experience a transformation that brings them closer together and strengthens their bond in ways they never thought possible. Through faith in Christ, families can break free from the chains of their past and create a new legacy of love, unity, and resilience that will impact generations to come. The true power of family lies not in the altars of dysfunction, but in the unbreakable covenant of love and grace that Christ offers to all who seek His healing touch. **Colossians** 2:14–15– *"He canceled the record of debt that stood against us with its legal demands. This He set aside, nailing it to the cross. He disarmed the rulers and authorities and put them to open shame."*

2 Corinthians 5:17–*"If anyone is in Christ, he is a new creation. The old has passed away; behold, the new has come."*

To **break ungodly altars:**

Identify the patterns. To break ungodly altars, we must first identify the patterns and behaviors in our lives that are not in alignment with God's will. By recognizing these areas of weakness, we can bring them before the Lord in prayer and ask for His strength and guidance to overcome them. Through the power of the Holy Spirit, we can break free from the chains of sin and walk in the victory that Christ has already won for us on the cross. Let us stand firm in our faith and trust that God is faithful to complete the good work He has started in us.

Renounce every covenant made knowingly or unknowingly. Let us surrender our hearts completely to God, renouncing any connections to darkness or evil influences. By confessing our sins and seeking God's forgiveness, we can experience true freedom and restoration in our relationship with Him. As we continue to walk in obedience and dependence on God, we can be confident that He will bring about transformation and renewal in our lives. Let us declare today that we belong to God alone and choose to live in accordance with His will, trusting in His unfailing love and grace.

Repent for family sins (Nehemiah 1:6–7). Let us also take responsibility for the sins of our families, following the example of Nehemiah, who confessed and repented for the sins of his ancestors. By acknowledging and repenting for any generational curses or patterns of sin in our families, we can break free from their hold and experience healing and restoration. May we humble ourselves before God, seeking His mercy and forgiveness not only for our own sins but also for those of our family members. In doing so, we can pave the way for God's blessings and favor to flow abundantly in our lives and in the lives of our loved ones.

Replace it with a new altar: prayer, worship, and dedication of your marriage and home to God. By building a new altar of prayer, worship, and dedication to God within our families, we can create a foundation of faith and strength that will protect us from the influence of past sins and curses. Through consistent prayer and worship, we can invite God's presence into our homes and marriages, allowing His blessings and favor to flow freely. Let us commit to breaking the chains of the past and creating a legacy of faith and righteousness for future generations to come.

11. **Reinforce** with ongoing prayer, communion, and the Word. Let us not grow weary in our pursuit of a strong and unwavering relationship with God, for it is through continual prayer, communion, and meditation on His Word that we will find the strength and guidance we need to overcome any obstacles that come our way. As we reinforce our commitment to God through these practices, we will see His hand at work in our lives, bringing peace, joy, and abundance to our marriages and homes. Let us stand firm in our faith, knowing that God is always with us, guiding us on the path to righteousness and blessing.

BUILDING A GODLY FAMILY ALTAR

Joshua declared, "As *for me and my house, we will serve the LORD.*" (Joshua 24:15)

Building a godly family altar is essential in creating a strong foundation for our homes. Just as Joshua made the declaration to serve the Lord in his household, we too must make a conscious decision to prioritize God in our families. By setting aside time for prayer, worship, and study of the Word together, we invite God's presence into our homes and allow Him to be the center of our lives. This intentional focus on God not only strengthens our own faith but also creates a legacy of spiritual growth and unity for generations to come. As we dedicate ourselves to building a godly family altar, we can trust that God will honor our commitment and bless our homes abundantly.

A godly altar is not about furniture; it is about **regular practices that invite God's presence into the family:**

Daily prayer as a couple or family. Reading and discussing scripture together, sharing testimonies of God's faithfulness, and worshiping together are all important components of a godly family altar. By prioritizing these practices, we demonstrate our love and devotion to God, setting an example for our children and grandchildren to follow. As we establish a foundation of faith in our homes, we can trust that God will continue to work in and through our families for His glory.

Communion in the home. Communion in the home is another powerful way to invite God's presence into the family altar. By partaking in the bread and wine together, we remember the sacrifice of Jesus and the forgiveness of sins that we have through Him. This act of communion not only strengthens our relationship with God but also deepens our bond as a family, reminding us of our unity in Christ. Together, these practices create a sacred space within our homes where we can seek God, grow in faith, and experience His presence in a tangible way.

Speaking blessings over children. Speaking blessings over children is another important aspect of creating a sacred and God-centered atmosphere in the home. By affirming and declaring positive words over our children, we are instilling confidence, love, and a sense of worth in them. It is a way to remind them of their identity as children of God and to encourage them to walk in the path that He has set for them. As we speak blessings over our children, we are inviting God's favor and protection into their lives, covering them with His love and grace. This practice not only nurtures their spiritual growth but also strengthens the family unit as a whole, creating a sense of unity and harmony rooted in God's love.

12. **Dedication of finances, home, and marriage to God.** Where ungodly altars once spoke death, godly altars now speak life. By dedicating our finances, home, and marriage to God, we are acknowledging His sovereignty and inviting

His presence to dwell in every aspect of our lives. Instead of relying on our own strength and understanding, we are choosing to trust in God's provision and guidance. As we build godly altars in our hearts and homes, we are paving the way for His blessings to flow abundantly and His love to reign supreme. The transformation from ungodly altars to godly altars is a powerful testimony of God's redemptive work in our lives, bringing forth new life and hope where there was once only darkness and despair.

REFLECTION QUESTIONS

What negative patterns do you see in your family line?

Have you identified any "altars" behaviors, addictions, or sayings that may be influencing your marriage?

What practical steps can you take to build a godly altar in your home today?

DECLARATION

I declare that the blood of Jesus has destroyed every ungodly altar in my family line. I renounce the practices of infidelity, abuse, poverty, rejection, and addiction. I will not repeat the patterns of my ancestors; I will establish a new altar of covenant in my marriage. As for me and my house, we will serve the Lord.

Moving forward, I will actively seek out and address any negative patterns that have been passed down through my family line. I will be vigilant in identifying and dismantling any altars of behavior, addiction, or sayings that may be negatively impacting my marriage. I will take practical steps to build a godly altar in my home by prioritizing communication, love, respect, and faith in God. I declare that every ungodly altar in my family line is broken by the blood of Jesus, and I will not be bound by the past. I renounce the destructive covenants of infidelity, abuse, poverty, rejection, and addiction, and I will strive to create a new legacy of love, faithfulness, and strength in my marriage. As for me and my house, we will serve the Lord and walk in His ways.

Prayer

Father, thank You that the cross of Jesus is greater than every altar of darkness. Today I bring my family line before You. I repent for the sins of my ancestors, and I renounce every ungodly covenant made on our behalf. By the blood of Jesus, I break the power of generational divorce, abuse, rejection, and poverty. Lord, I dedicate my marriage, my children, and my home as a living altar to You. Let Your presence dwell with us, and let Your blessing flow through generations to come. In Jesus' name, amen.

PART III

Healing And Restoration

CHAPTER 9

QUESTIONS OF REMARRIAGE

Navigating Second Chances and Sacred Boundaries

Perhaps no subject creates as much confusion and guilt in the hearts of believers as the question of remarriage. For some, the fear is that remarriage after divorce is always adultery, forever placing them outside of God's blessing. For others, the assumption is that once divorced, remarriage is simply the next step forward, with little reflection on what God's Word teaches. Between these extremes lies a biblical path—one that upholds the sanctity of covenant while extending the grace of Christ to those who have stumbled.

In exploring the topic of remarriage after divorce, it is crucial to approach it with humility, seeking wisdom from God's Word and guidance from the Holy Spirit. It is important to remember that each situation is unique and requires discernment and prayer. The goal should always be to seek healing and restoration in Christ, allowing His grace to lead us in making decisions that honor Him. Let us delve deeper into the Scriptures and seek God's wisdom as we navigate the complexities of remarriage after divorce. While it is important to seek guidance from God's Word and the Holy Spirit, it is also important to consider the biblical teachings on divorce and remarriage, which may provide clarity on the sanctity of marriage vows. It is essential to balance grace and truth in addressing this sensitive issue. Some relevant Bible scriptures on marriage in the NKJV include Ephesians 5:25, which states, "Husbands, love your wives, just as Christ also loved the church and gave Himself for her." Another scripture is 1 Corinthians 7:2: "But because of sexual immorality, let each man have his own wife, and let each woman have her own husband." These verses emphasize the importance of love and fidelity in marriage according to God's design. Through prayer and seeking wisdom from God's Word, we can navigate the complexities of relationships with grace and truth.

WHEN COVENANT ENDS

The first truth we must affirm is that marriage is a covenant designed to last for life. Jesus' teaching, as we saw, is clear: what God has joined, man must not separate. Yet both Jesus and Paul also acknowledge that sometimes covenant is broken—by sexual immorality, by abandonment, by violence, and by treachery. When a covenant is desecrated, the innocent party is not bound.

This means that remarriage, in certain circumstances, is not adultery but restoration. A widow or widower may remarry freely, Paul says, as long as it is "in the Lord" (1 Cor. 7:39). A man or woman betrayed by adultery may remarry, for the "one flesh" union has already been violated. And the believer abandoned by an unbelieving spouse is, in Paul's words, "not enslaved," free to live in peace (1 Cor. 7:15).

It is crucial here to remember that God does not desire His children to live in perpetual chains.

In fact, He offers freedom and restoration to those who have been wronged in their marriages. This is not to say that divorce should be taken lightly, but rather that God's heart is for His children to live in peace and wholeness. As we navigate the complexities of marriage and divorce, it is important to seek God's guidance and wisdom, trusting that He can bring beauty from brokenness and redemption from pain.

Where covenant has been broken beyond repair, remarriage is not rebellion but grace.

It is a recognition of God's ability to bring new life and healing to those who have suffered in their previous relationships. Remarriage can be a symbol of God's faithfulness and restoration, a testament to His power to redeem even the most broken of situations. As we move forward in faith and obedience, we can trust that God will continue to work in our lives, bringing beauty from ashes and joy from mourning. Let us embrace the grace and freedom that God offers, knowing that He is always faithful to His children.

WHEN REMARRIAGE BECOMES ADULTERY

But we must also confront Jesus' stark warning: "Whoever divorces his wife, except for sexual immorality, and marries another, commits adultery" (Matt. 19:9). Here lies the sobering truth: not all remarriages are blessed. When someone divorces for unbiblical reasons—for personal convenience, for boredom, for "irreconcilable differences" that are really hardness of heart—remarriage does not erase the sin. It compounds it.

The pain and brokenness of divorce are not magically erased by a new marriage. Instead, the cycle of sin continues as the remarried couple lives in adultery. This is a difficult truth to swallow, especially in a culture that often celebrates second chances and new beginnings. But as Christians, we are called to uphold the sanctity of marriage and the seriousness of the vows we make before God. We must strive to honor those vows, even when it means facing the consequences of past mistakes.

This is where many stumble, for the words of Christ are sharp. Wrongful remarriage is sin. It must be confessed. It must be repented of. But here is the good news: it is not a life sentence of condemnation. Adultery is not the unforgivable sin. What begins in rebellion can, through repentance, become a covenant sanctified by grace.

It is through the grace and mercy of God that we are able to find forgiveness and redemption, even in the midst of our brokenness. It is a journey of humility and surrender, of acknowledging our wrongs and seeking reconciliation with God and our spouse. It is a process of healing and restoration, of learning to walk in obedience and faithfulness to the vows we have made. Though the road may be difficult and the path may be narrow, we can trust in the promise that God's love and forgiveness are greater than our sin.

THE WEIGHT OF REPENTANCE

What, then, does repentance look like for someone who has remarried wrongly? It is not to abandon the new spouse and return to the first. In fact, Deuteronomy 24 explicitly forbids such a return. Repentance is not a new act of betrayal. Instead, repentance is a confession: "Lord, I sinned when I entered this covenant wrongly. Forgive me." And having confessed, the believer must now honor the covenant they are in, remaining faithful to the spouse they have married.

God does not delight in the repeated breaking of vows. He is a Redeemer, not a destroyer. Once a new covenant is made, even in sin, His desire is to forgive the sin and sanctify the covenant. Just as He took Rahab the harlot and grafted her into His holy lineage, so He takes broken covenants and, through repentance, writes redemption into their story.

Repentance is not just a one-time event but a continual turning away from sin and back to God. It requires a change of heart and a commitment to living in accordance with His will. It is a process of transformation, of becoming more like Christ and less like our sinful selves. And through this process, God's grace and mercy are poured out upon us, cleansing us from our sins and restoring us to a right relationship with Him. In His eyes, we are not defined by our past mistakes, but by His love and forgiveness.

STORIES OF REDEMPTION

I remember counseling a man who had divorced his wife in anger and married another woman out of passion, not prayer. For years he lived under a cloud of guilt, believing he was in perpetual adultery. But as he came to understand God's Word, he confessed his sin with tears. He and his new wife consecrated their marriage before God, determined to walk in holiness from that day forward. That marriage, once born in rebellion, became a testimony of redemption. Today, they minister to other couples, teaching faithfulness out of their own story of failure and grace.

This is the gospel: not that sin is minimized, but that grace is maximized. Where sin abounds, grace abounds more (Rom. 5:20).

THE SAMARITAN WOMAN'S HOPE

Consider Jesus' encounter with the Samaritan woman in John 4. She had been married five times and was now living with a man who was not her husband. By every standard, her life was a picture of broken covenants. Yet Jesus did not condemn her. He offered her living water. He revealed Himself to her as Messiah. He entrusted her to become the first evangelist in her city.

In this powerful story, we see how Jesus met the Samaritan woman in the midst of her brokenness and shame, and instead of judging her, He extended grace and love. He saw beyond her failures and recognized her potential to be a messenger of hope to others. This is a beautiful example of how grace can transform even the most hopeless situations into opportunities for redemption and new beginnings. The Samaritan woman's story reminds us that no matter how far we have strayed or how many mistakes we have made, there is always room for grace to abound and for our lives to be transformed by the love of God.

If Jesus could redeem her broken story, can He not redeem ours? Divorce and remarriage do not disqualify anyone from His grace or His calling. With repentance, the past can be covered, and the present sanctified.

GRACE AND RESPONSIBILITY

Still, grace never removes responsibility. Those who have walked through divorce and remarriage must carry their story with humility. They should not boast of "moving on" lightly but acknowledge the pain and consequences of broken vows. Their testimony should not be one of dismissal but of redemption.

Their lives should reflect a deep gratitude for the grace that has covered their past mistakes and a commitment to live in a way that honors the covenant of marriage. It is a delicate balance of receiving God's grace while also taking responsibility for the choices that led to the brokenness. By doing so, they can truly experience the transforming power of God's love in their lives and be a living testimony to His faithfulness.

Pastors and churches must also hold the balance. We must not shackle believers under lifelong condemnation for past mistakes, nor must we normalize divorce and remarriage as if covenant means little. The balance is the cross: holiness and mercy, justice and grace, truth and love.

It is through this balance that we can truly minister to those who are struggling in their marriages, offering them both the truth of God's word and the love and grace that He extends to all who seek Him. As pastors and church leaders, we must be willing to walk alongside those who are facing challenges in their marriages, offering them support, guidance, and prayer as they navigate the difficult waters of marital brokenness. By upholding the sanctity of marriage while also extending God's grace and forgiveness, we can help couples find healing and restoration in their relationships, ultimately bringing glory to God through the redemption of their marriages.

A PROPHETIC PICTURE: THE NEW COVENANT

In many ways, remarriage–when sanctified by repentance–becomes a prophetic picture of the new covenant itself. The old covenant was broken by sin. It had to be set aside. But through Christ, a new covenant was established, not because God had failed, but because humanity had. This new covenant is not illegitimate; it is glorious. It is sealed in blood, empowered by the Spirit, and filled with grace.

Through remarriage, couples have the opportunity to experience a tangible representation of this new covenant. Just as God forgives and restores His people, couples who choose to repent and reconcile can experience a renewed and transformed relationship. This act of forgiveness and restoration not only brings healing to the couple but also serves as a powerful testimony to others of God's redemptive power in relationships. Just as the new covenant is sealed in blood, empowered by the Spirit, and filled with grace, so too can remarriage be a beautiful reflection of God's love and mercy in the midst of brokenness.

So it is, in a lesser way, with remarriage. When sin has broken the first, God can redeem the second. The point is not that divorce is good, but that grace is greater.

In the midst of our brokenness and failures, God's grace is always available to bring restoration and redemption. Just as He forgives our sins and offers us a fresh start, He can also heal and renew a remarriage that has been broken by past mistakes. It is a testament to His love and mercy that even in the midst of our brokenness, He can bring beauty and wholeness out of the ashes.

CLOSING REFLECTION

Remarriage after divorce is not a simple yes or no. It is a matter of covenant, sin, repentance, and grace. Some remarriages are holy from the beginning, following biblical release. Others are born in sin, but repentance can sanctify them. All must be approached with humility, prayer, and a deep reverence for the God who hates divorce but delights in redemption.

In the end, the question is not merely, *"Can I remarry?"* The deeper question is, *"Can this covenant I now live in glorify Christ?"* If the answer is yes–through repentance, faithfulness, and holiness–then even the most broken story can become a testimony of grace.

CHAPTER 10

BOUNDARIES, FORGIVENESS, AND RESTORATION

Rebuilding Trust on the Road to Wholeness

MARRIAGE, LIKE ANY COVENANT, THRIVES within the framework of healthy boundaries. A boundary is not a wall of separation but a fence of protection, a marker that defines where one life ends and the other begins and how those lives intertwine without devouring each other. In the absence of boundaries, marriages drift into chaos: trust erodes, intimacy falters, and love becomes vulnerable to intrusion. Yet even when boundaries are crossed, the gospel gives us a pathway to forgiveness and restoration by which marriages can be healed.

WHY BOUNDARIES MATTER IN COVENANT LOVE

From the very beginning, God established boundaries. In Eden, Adam and Eve were given freedom within limits: *"You may surely eat of every tree… but of the tree of the knowledge of good and evil you shall not eat"* (Gen. 2:16–17).

These boundaries were meant to protect and preserve the relationship between God and humanity. Similarly, in marriage, boundaries are essential for maintaining the health and strength of the relationship. Without boundaries, there is no structure or order, leading to temptation, confusion and conflict. Just as God set boundaries for Adam and Eve in the garden, couples must establish boundaries in their marriage to ensure that their love remains strong and secure.

Boundaries protect relationships with God, just as they protect covenants in marriage. Boundaries help to define expectations, create a sense of safety, and establish mutual respect between partners. By clearly communicating and upholding boundaries, couples can prevent misunderstandings, build trust, and cultivate a deeper connection with each other. Ultimately, boundaries in marriage serve to honor the sacred commitment made between two individuals and strengthen the bond they share. Just as God's boundaries were set out of love and care for Adam and Eve, couples can set boundaries in their marriage out of love and respect for each other.

In marriage, boundaries serve three purposes: they protect trust, preserve dignity, and foster growth within the relationship. Trust is the foundation of any healthy marriage, and boundaries help to maintain that trust by ensuring that both partners feel safe and secure in the relationship. By respecting each other's boundaries, couples show that they value and honor each other's feelings and needs. This not only preserves the dignity of each individual but also strengthens the bond between partners. Additionally, boundaries create space for personal growth and self-discovery within the marriage. When each partner is free to express their needs and desires, they can continue to evolve and develop both individually and as a couple. Overall, boundaries in marriage are essential for creating a strong and lasting partnership built on love, respect, and understanding.

A husband who sets a boundary that he will not confide in other women the way he does with his wife is not limiting himself; he is safeguarding intimacy. By establishing this boundary, he is showing his commitment to his marriage and prioritizing the emotional connection he shares with his spouse. This not only fosters trust and security within the relationship but also allows both partners to feel valued and respected. Boundaries in marriage serve as a guide for how each individual wants to be treated and what is acceptable within the partnership. When these boundaries are communicated and respected, it creates a healthy dynamic where both partners feel heard and understood. This ultimately leads to a stronger and more fulfilling relationship where both individuals can thrive and grow together.

A wife who insists that finances remain transparent is not distrusting; she is preserving trust. This transparency allows both partners to feel secure in knowing where their money is going and how it is being managed. It also helps to prevent misunderstandings or conflicts that can arise from financial secrecy. By setting this boundary, the wife is communicating her need for open communication and honesty in the relationship, which ultimately strengthens the bond between her and her partner. In return, the husband's willingness to adhere to this boundary shows his respect for her feelings and his commitment to maintaining a healthy and trusting partnership.

Boundaries are not chains; they are anchors of covenant love. Boundaries in a relationship serve as a foundation for trust and respect, allowing both partners to feel valued and understood. By establishing clear expectations around financial transparency, the couple is creating a safe space for open dialogue and shared decision-making. This mutual understanding fosters a deeper connection and a sense of partnership, where both individuals feel heard and supported in their shared goals and values. Ultimately, boundaries help to strengthen the bond between partners and cultivate a relationship built on trust and mutual respect.

ILLUSTRATION

Think of a garden. Without fences, wild animals trample the plants. Without pathways, even the gardener's feet crush the flowers.

Boundaries serve as the fences and pathways in a relationship, protecting and guiding the growth of love and understanding. Just as a garden needs clear boundaries to thrive, so too does a partnership require mutual respect and communication to flourish. By establishing and maintaining healthy boundaries, couples can nurture a strong and resilient connection that withstands the challenges of life's unpredictable seasons. Just as a well-tended garden blooms with beauty and vitality, so too can a relationship blossom and thrive when nurtured with love, respect, and clear boundaries.

Boundaries do not choke the garden; they allow it to flourish. So it is with marriage.

Setting boundaries in a relationship is not about restricting freedom or stifling individuality, but rather about creating a safe and respectful space for both partners to grow and thrive. Just as a garden needs regular care and attention to flourish, so too does a marriage require ongoing communication and compromise to stay healthy and strong. By clearly defining boundaries and respecting each other's needs and boundaries, couples can cultivate a deep and lasting love that withstands the test of time. Just as a well-tended garden can weather storms and still bloom with beauty, so too can a marriage withstand challenges and continue to flourish when built on a foundation of mutual respect and understanding.

COMMON BOUNDARIES THAT PROTECT MARRIAGE

Boundaries take many forms: emotional, spiritual, physical, financial, and even verbal. For example, couples may agree never to insult one another in anger, never to make unilateral financial decisions, and never to threaten divorce as a weapon in conflict. These boundaries are not legalistic rules but relational safeguards.

They serve as guidelines to protect the sanctity of the marriage and ensure that both partners feel safe and respected in the relationship. By establishing and respecting these boundaries, couples can navigate disagreements and challenges with grace and maturity, ultimately strengthening their bond and deepening their connection. In essence, boundaries create a sense of security and trust within the marriage, allowing both partners to feel valued and supported in their journey together.

They create a safe and respectful environment where both partners can thrive and grow together.

Boundaries also help to establish clear communication and expectations within the relationship, preventing misunderstandings and conflicts from arising. When both partners are aware of and respect each other's boundaries, they can avoid unnecessary tension and friction in their interactions. This mutual understanding and respect for boundaries foster a sense of harmony and balance in the marriage, enabling both individuals to express themselves freely and authentically without fear of judgment or rejection. In essence, boundaries serve as a foundation for a healthy and fulfilling marriage, allowing both partners to feel secure and confident in their love for each other.

By setting and respecting these boundaries, couples can protect their marriage from harm and strengthen their bond. Just as a garden needs boundaries to flourish, so too does a marriage require boundaries to thrive. It is through these common boundaries that couples can navigate the ups and downs of life together, building a strong foundation for their relationship to weather any storm.

In pastoral counseling, I have often seen couples restored simply by reestablishing clear boundaries. A husband who spent hours scrolling through pornography broke his wife's trust, not only by what he viewed but also by the secrecy surrounding it. When he agreed to accountability software and open communication, a new boundary was set that slowly rebuilt safety and trust in their relationship. Similarly, a wife who constantly criticized her husband in front of others learned to set boundaries around her words and actions, leading to a newfound respect and admiration for her partner. By setting and respecting boundaries, couples can create a safe and secure environment where love and connection can flourish.

A wife who allowed her mother to dictate every household decision learned to set a boundary: "I love you, Mom, but I will honor my husband first." That boundary saved her marriage.

Setting boundaries in relationships is crucial for maintaining a healthy dynamic and ensuring mutual respect. It allows individuals to establish their own needs and limits while also considering the needs of their partner. By clearly communicating and upholding these boundaries, couples can navigate conflicts more effectively and cultivate a stronger bond built on trust and understanding. In essence, boundaries serve as the foundation for a successful and fulfilling relationship, where both parties feel valued and respected.

WHEN BOUNDARIES ARE VIOLATED

But what happens when boundaries are crossed? Here we meet the painful reality of betrayal. Jesus Himself spoke of offenses: *"It is impossible but that offenses will come"* (Luke 17:1, KJV). Even in covenant, sin intrudes. A harsh word, a hidden bank account, an adulterous affair—

these are not mere mistakes, but violations of sacred trust.

When boundaries are violated, the trust that was once established is shattered, leaving behind a sense of betrayal and hurt. It can feel like a deep wound that may take time to heal, if it ever does. The violation of boundaries can lead to feelings of anger, resentment, and even a loss of respect for the other person. It can be difficult to move past these violations and rebuild the trust that was broken. In order to address boundary violations, it is important for both parties to communicate openly and honestly about what happened, how it made them feel, and what steps can be taken to prevent it from happening again in the future.

When boundaries are violated, couples stand at a crossroads. One path leads to bitterness, distance, and eventual dissolution. The other leads through the valley of forgiveness toward the possibility of restoration and a stronger, healthier relationship. It requires both parties to acknowledge their role in the violation and be willing to make changes to prevent it from happening again. By setting clear boundaries, communicating effectively, and working together to rebuild trust, couples can overcome boundary violations and strengthen their connection. It is not an easy journey, but with commitment and effort, it is possible to move past the hurt and create a more secure and fulfilling relationship.

The choice is not easy, but it is crucial. It requires a willingness to confront uncomfortable truths and address underlying issues that may have contributed to the boundary violation. Both partners must be open to exploring their own vulnerabilities and insecurities, as well as understanding the impact of their actions on the other person. This process can be painful and challenging, but it is necessary for true healing and growth to occur. By facing these difficult truths together, couples can emerge stronger and more resilient, with a deeper understanding and appreciation for each other. The choice to embark on this journey is a brave one, and the rewards of a restored and strengthened relationship are well worth the effort.

THE NATURE OF FORGIVENESS

Forgiveness is not denial. It does not say, "It didn't matter," or "It didn't hurt." Forgiveness names the sin for what it is and then releases the offender from the debt. Jesus modeled this at the cross: *"Father, forgive them, for they know not what they do"* (Luke 23:34). He did not excuse the crucifixion; He forgave in spite of it.

Forgiveness requires acknowledging the pain and wrongdoing but choosing to let go of the anger and resentment that can poison relationships. It is a conscious decision to release the burden of holding onto past hurts and to move forward with a spirit of grace and compassion. By choosing to forgive, we open the door to healing and reconciliation, allowing for the possibility of a renewed and transformed relationship. Just as Jesus demonstrated on the cross, forgiveness has the power to bring about redemption and restoration, paving the way for a future filled with love and understanding.

In marriage, forgiveness is not a one-time event but a continual practice. Spouses wound each other, sometimes daily. Yet the covenant endures when forgiveness flows. Paul commands, *"Be kind to one another, tenderhearted, forgiving one another, as God in Christ forgave you"* (Eph. 4:32).

ILLUSTRATION

Forgiveness is like clearing debris from a river. If stones of offense are left to pile up, the water of love is dammed. Forgiveness removes the stones, allowing the river to flow again.

It is a deliberate choice to let go of resentment and bitterness and to extend grace and mercy to our spouse, just as God has done for us. It requires humility, vulnerability, and a willingness to move forward in love. By practicing forgiveness in marriage, we not only strengthen our bond with our spouse, but we also reflect the forgiveness and grace that we have received from God. Just as the river flows freely when the debris is cleared, so too can love and understanding flourish in a marriage where forgiveness is continually practiced.

FORGIVENESS VERSUS RESTORATION

It is vital to distinguish forgiveness from restoration. Forgiveness can be granted instantly—a heart releasing bitterness. But restoration requires time, repentance, and trust rebuilt. A man who confesses adultery may be forgiven by his wife in a moment, but restoration of intimacy may take years. Forgiveness is a gift; restoration is a process.

This is why quick counsel like "just forgive and move on" is shallow and even harmful.

Such counsel overlooks the complexity and depth of the wounds that need to be healed in order for true restoration to occur. It also fails to acknowledge the importance of boundaries and accountability in rebuilding trust. Without these essential components, forgiveness alone cannot fully repair the damage done to a relationship. Therefore, it is crucial for couples to understand the difference between forgiveness and restoration and to actively work towards both in order to truly heal and strengthen their marriage.

Real restoration requires confession, repentance, accountability, and often pastoral or therapeutic support. It is slow work, but holy work.

BIBLICAL PORTRAITS OF FORGIVENESS AND RESTORATION

The story of Hosea and Gomer is one of Scripture's most powerful pictures. Gomer betrayed Hosea repeatedly, chasing after other lovers. Yet God commanded Hosea to redeem her, not because she deserved it, but because his love was to be a mirror of God's covenant with unfaithful Israel. This does not mean every betrayed spouse must return—but it reveals the possibility of restoration through supernatural love.

Likewise, Peter denied Jesus three times. Yet Jesus restored him on the shores of Galilee: *"Do you love Me? Feed My sheep."* (John 21). Forgiveness restored relationships; trust empowers God-given missions.

WHEN FORGIVENESS IS NOT ENOUGH

There are times when forgiveness does not lead to reconciliation—when abuse continues, repentance is absent, or boundaries are repeatedly trampled. In such cases, forgiveness may free the victim's heart, but the restoration of marriage may not be possible due to ongoing harm and lack of genuine change. In these situations, it is important for the betrayed spouse to prioritize their own safety and well-being, seeking support from trusted friends, family, or professionals. It is crucial to set boundaries and protect oneself from further harm, even if reconciliation is not possible. Ultimately, forgiveness is a personal journey that can bring healing and freedom, even in the absence of restored relationships.

God does not call His children to remain in perpetual cycles of destruction. In those instances, forgiveness releases the offender to God's justice, while the victim steps into peace.

It is a difficult and often painful process but choosing to forgive can lead to a sense of liberation and inner peace. By letting go of resentment and anger, the betrayed spouse can begin to move forward and rebuild their life. While the scars of betrayal may never fully disappear, forgiveness can help to lessen their impact and allow for personal growth and healing. Ultimately, forgiveness is a gift we give ourselves, allowing us to break free from the chains of the past and embrace a brighter future.

THE PROPHETIC ROLE OF BOUNDARIES AND FORGIVENESS

In a generation where marriage is fragile, couples who practice boundaries and forgiveness become prophetic witnesses. They demonstrate to the world that grace and discipline are just as important to sustaining a covenant as romance. A marriage where boundaries are respected and forgiveness flows is like a lighthouse–steady in storms, guiding others toward hope.

Boundaries provide a framework for healthy communication and mutual respect within a relationship. They establish clear expectations and consequences, helping to prevent misunderstandings and conflicts. When boundaries are consistently enforced, they create a sense of safety and security, allowing both partners to feel valued and understood. In addition, forgiveness plays a crucial role in maintaining a strong and lasting bond between two individuals. By letting go of past hurts and resentments, couples can move forward with a renewed sense of trust and intimacy. Together, boundaries and forgiveness form the foundation of a thriving marriage, serving as a beacon of hope for others seeking to build a lasting partnership.

CLOSING REFLECTION

Boundaries guard covenant. Forgiveness heals breaches. Restoration rebuilds trust. These three together create marriages that not only survive but also testify to the glory of Christ and His church. The question for every couple is not whether they will offend one another, but whether they will choose the path of forgiveness and restoration when boundaries are broken.

Marriage, after all, is not the union of two perfect people, but the covenant of two sinners learning to love as Christ loved—with truth, with grace, and with the hope of redemption. Choosing to forgive and restore within a marriage is a powerful testament to the transformative power of love and grace. It is in these moments of vulnerability and humility that true growth and healing can occur. By following the example of Christ in our relationships, we can build marriages that reflect His unconditional love and redemption. As imperfect beings, we must constantly strive to extend forgiveness and seek restoration, knowing that it is through these acts that we can truly experience the beauty and depth of a Christ-centered partnership.

CHAPTER 11

The Role of the Church as a Healing Community

Embracing the Broken and Restoring Hope

WHEN MARRIAGES COLLAPSE AND FAMILIES shatter, the reverberations do not stop at the door of the home. They shake the church as well. Every pastor has felt it: the couple who once sat side by side now sit separately, or not at all; the children who once ran joyfully to Sunday School now withdraw in confusion; the ministry team fractured because two of its members are in conflict at home. Divorce does not remain private. It bleeds into the body of Christ.

The church must step up as a healing community in these times of brokenness. It is not enough to simply offer prayers and platitudes; action must be taken to support and restore those who are hurting. This may involve providing counseling services, hosting support groups, or simply being a listening ear for those in need. The church has a unique opportunity to show God's love and grace in these moments of crisis, and it is essential that we rise to the occasion. By coming together as a community, we can help mend the wounds caused by broken relationships and bring healing to those who are suffering.

The question is not whether divorce will touch the church, but how the church will respond when it does. Will we become a community that condemns or a community that heals? Will we perpetuate shame, or will we embody the grace and truth of Christ?

It is crucial that we approach the topic of divorce with compassion and understanding, recognizing that every situation is complex and unique. We must resist the temptation to pass judgment and instead offer support and guidance to those who are going through this difficult time. As followers of Christ, we are called to love one another unconditionally, just as He loves us. Let us be a beacon of hope and healing for those who are hurting, showing them the love and grace that Christ has shown us. "Do not judge, or you too will be judged. For in the same way you judge others, you will be judged, and with the measure you use, it will be measured to you." – Matthew 7:1-2 (NKJV)

As we navigate the delicate issue of divorce, let us remember these words and refrain from passing harsh judgment on those going through this painful experience. Instead, let us offer them the same grace and understanding that Christ has shown us. Let our actions be guided by love and compassion, rather than condemnation.

THE CHURCH AS COVENANT WITNESS

From the beginning, marriage has been a public covenant. In ancient Israel, marriages were celebrated at the city gates, in the presence of elders and community. The church, as the gathered people of God, continues this role. When a couple says, "I do," before witnesses, the church is not a silent bystander but an active covenant witness.

The church is called to support and uphold the marriage covenant, not just in times of celebration but also in times of struggle and hardship. Just as God is faithful to his covenant with his people, the church is called to reflect that faithfulness in its support of married couples. This means offering guidance, encouragement, and resources to help couples navigate the challenges that inevitably arise in marriage. By being a covenant witness, the church can help couples stay true to their vows and experience the fullness of God's love and grace in their relationship.

This means that the church also bears responsibility when covenants are broken. Not responsibility for the sin itself, but responsibility to shepherd, to discipline, to heal, and to restore. Paul exhorted the Galatians: *"Brothers, if anyone is caught in any transgression, you who are spiritual should restore him in a spirit of gentleness."* (Gal. 6:1). The church is not a courtroom pronouncing sentence; it is a hospital tending the wounded.

It is through this restoration process that the church can truly demonstrate the love and forgiveness of God. Just as Christ forgave us of our sins, the church must also extend that same grace and mercy to those who have fallen short. By walking alongside those who have broken their covenants, the church can help guide them back to a place of wholeness and reconciliation. This is not an easy task, but it is a crucial one in order to uphold the sanctity of marriage and the importance of keeping one's word.

THE WOUNDED IN OUR MIDST

In every congregation, there are men and women silently suffering the aftershocks of divorce. Some wear their wounds openly, asking for prayer. Others hide in shame, fearing judgment. Still others pretend all is well, while their homes collapse in secret.

It is imperative for the church to create a safe and welcoming space for these individuals to heal and find support. It is essential for the church community to offer compassion, understanding, and practical assistance to those who are struggling with the aftermath of divorce. Only by extending love and grace to the wounded in our midst can we truly embody the teachings of Christ and fulfill our mission as a beacon of hope and healing in a broken world. For example, a woman who recently went through a divorce may feel isolated and alone in her pain, hesitant to reach out for help. By creating support groups or counseling services specifically tailored for individuals navigating divorce, the church can provide a safe space for her to share her struggles and receive guidance on how to navigate this difficult time. Through acts of kindness, listening ears, and genuine care, the church community can offer practical assistance such as helping with childcare, providing meals, or offering financial support to alleviate some.

CASE STUDY

I recall a young mother who came faithfully to church every Sunday, always smiling, always serving. Yet behind her smile was a husband who berated her nightly and children who wept themselves to sleep. She feared speaking up, convinced that divorce would mark her as "disqualified" in the eyes of the church. When the truth finally emerged, she said, "I didn't think the church was a safe place for broken people."

Her words should pierce us. The church is meant to be the safest place for the broken. Christ Himself declared: *"The Spirit of the Lord is upon Me... He has sent me to bind up the brokenhearted."* (Luke 4:18). If His Spirit is upon us, should not His church bind up the brokenhearted too?

SHEPHERDING THROUGH MARITAL CRISIS

A healing church does not wait for marriages to collapse before acting. It shepherds couples proactively, providing premarital counseling, offering marriage enrichment courses, and creating a culture of support and accountability within the congregation. When a marital crisis does arise, the church should be a place of refuge and restoration, not judgment and condemnation. By following Christ's example of compassion and grace, the church can truly be a beacon of hope for those who are struggling in their relationships.

Premarital Counseling: Preparing couples to understand covenant, boundaries, and the spiritual realities of family altars. By helping couples establish a strong foundation based on mutual respect, communication, and shared values, premarital counseling can set them up for a lifetime of love and commitment. It is important for couples to understand the significance of their marriage vows and the responsibilities that come with them. By addressing potential issues and providing tools for navigating challenges, premarital counseling can help couples build a solid and enduring relationship that honors God.

Marital Discipleship: Offering teaching, retreats, and small groups where couples can strengthen their covenant together. Marital Discipleship offers a supportive community where couples can continue to grow and deepen their relationship after the wedding day. Through teaching, retreats, and small groups, couples can learn how to apply biblical principles to their marriage and navigate the ups and downs of life together. By investing in their relationship and seeking guidance from experienced mentors, couples can build a strong foundation that will sustain them through the years to come.

Crisis Intervention: When conflict arises, stepping in not as judges but as mediators, offering biblical counsel and prayer. This approach allows couples to address issues in a healthy and constructive manner, rather than letting them fester and grow into larger problems. By seeking intervention during times of crisis, couples can work through their issues with a supportive community by their side, strengthening their bond and deepening their commitment to each other. Ultimately, discipleship provides couples with the tools and support they need to weather the storms of life together, emerging stronger and more united than ever before.

Restorative Discipline: Confronting unrepentant sin (adultery, abuse, abandonment) with both truth and love, always aiming at repentance, not shame. Restorative discipline in relationships involves addressing serious issues such as adultery, abuse, or abandonment with a balance of truth and love. The goal is not to shame the other person but to guide them towards repentance and reconciliation. By confronting unrepentant sin in a supportive and loving manner, couples can rebuild trust and strengthen their bond, ultimately creating a healthier and more united partnership. This approach allows couples to address challenges head-on and move forward together with a deeper understanding and commitment to each other.

The church's goal is not merely to preserve appearances but to protect holiness and nurture healing. This approach also emphasizes the importance of seeking guidance from a spiritual leader or counselor who can provide wisdom and support throughout the reconciliation process. By incorporating prayer, scripture, and community into the process, couples can find strength and encouragement as they navigate the difficult journey towards forgiveness and restoration. Ultimately, the church's role is to walk alongside couples in their journey towards healing and restoration, offering grace, support, and accountability along the way.

THE CHURCH AS FAMILY FOR THE FATHERLESS

Divorce often leaves children adrift. Here the church must rise as a spiritual family. Psalm 68:6 declares, *"God sets the lonely in families."* The local church is that family.

It is a place where fatherless children can find love, support, and guidance as they navigate the challenges of growing up without a father figure. The church can provide positive male role models, mentorship programs, and opportunities for children to experience the love and care of a father figure in a safe and nurturing environment. By stepping in to fill the void left by absent fathers, the church can help to break the cycle of fatherlessness and provide children with the support they need to thrive and succeed in life.

Practical expressions include:

Spiritual fathers and mothers **mentoring** children of divorce. By fostering a sense of community and belonging, the church can create a supportive environment where fatherless children feel valued and loved. Through mentorship programs and guidance from spiritual fathers and mothers, children of divorce can receive the guidance and encouragement they need to navigate the challenges they face. By offering a positive and stable influence in their lives, the church can play a crucial role in helping these children build a strong foundation for their future.

Sunday school teachers being more than **instructors**, and Sunday schools becoming safe places for devastated children. These teachers can provide not only academic lessons but also emotional support and guidance, serving as role models for children who may not have a father figure at home. By showing care and compassion, these teachers can help fill the void left by absent parents and create a sense of security and belonging for these children. In this way, the church can truly be a source of healing and restoration for fatherless children, offering them the love and support they need to thrive despite their circumstances.

Youth ministries that acknowledge the **realities of broken homes** without stigmatizing those who come from them. By providing a safe and nurturing environment, these youth ministries can empower children to overcome their adversities and reach their full potential. By offering mentorship and guidance, they can instill values of resilience, perseverance, and self-worth in these children, helping them navigate the challenges of growing up without a father figure. Through their unconditional love and support, these ministries can make a lasting impact on the lives of fatherless children, showing them that they are valued and capable of achieving great things.

ILLUSTRATION

A teenage boy once told me, "I only have one real dad, but I feel like I have five spiritual dads in this church." That is the church functioning as a healing community, filling the gaps left by broken covenants.

These spiritual fathers within the church provide mentorship, guidance, and a sense of belonging to these fatherless children, helping to shape their character and instill a sense of purpose in their lives. By stepping in to support and nurture these children, the church not only offers them a sense of stability and security but also helps them develop the skills and confidence needed to overcome the obstacles they may face. The impact of these ministries goes beyond just providing material or emotional support; they are truly changing the trajectory of these children's lives for the better.

THE TENSION OF TRUTH AND GRACE

The church often errs on one of two extremes. In some communities, truth is emphasized to the point of cruelty: divorced believers are stigmatized, forbidden from serving, treated as though they carry a permanent scarlet letter. In others, grace is emphasized to the point of permissiveness: divorce is never confronted, remarriage is treated casually, and covenant loses its sacredness.

But Christ came "full of grace and truth" (John 1:14). The church must reflect both. We must preach the covenant boldly–that marriage is sacred, lifelong, and holy. Yet we must also minister grace deeply– that failure is not final, and redemption is possible.

PROPHETIC WARNING

A church that abandons truth becomes powerless. A church that abandons grace becomes merciless. Only when both are held together can the church truly heal.

DIVORCE, REMARRIAGE, AND MINISTRY

One of the most difficult pastoral questions is whether divorced and remarried believers can serve in ministry. Some traditions disqualify them entirely. Others treat it as irrelevant. The healing church must walk wisely.

If a believer divorced for unbiblical reasons, remarried without repentance, and now seeks leadership, the church must require confession and consecration. The past cannot be ignored. But neither should the blood of Christ be denied. Once sin is confessed and covenant honored in the present, such believers can serve with humility, often bringing unique empathy to others in pain.

Remember Peter: he denied Christ yet was restored and became a pillar of the church. Failure does not disqualify forever. Repentance restores.

PROPHETIC PICTURE: THE CHURCH AS BRIDE

Marriage points to Christ and His church. Divorce distorts that picture. But here is the mystery: the church itself has often been unfaithful to Christ, yet He has not divorced her. He disciplines, He restores, and He redeems. In the same way, the church must embody His patient love.

When the church walks with couples through betrayal, forgiveness, and restoration, it becomes a living parable of Christ's love for His bride. The healing of marriages is not just pastoral care; it is gospel proclamation.

A COMMUNITY OF NEW ALTARS

Earlier we spoke of family altars. The church is itself a communal altar – a place where broken covenants are brought before God and new beginnings are birthed. When divorced believers are welcomed, not shunned; when children of broken homes are embraced, not pitied; when couples on the brink are prayed for, not gossiped about—the church becomes an altar of healing.

This is what Paul envisioned when he wrote to the Ephesians about the church being a temple, built together as a dwelling place for God's Spirit (Eph. 2:21–22). A temple where fractured stones are not discarded but fitted together into something glorious.

CLOSING REFLECTION

The role of the church is not to condemn the broken but to redeem them. It is not to deny the pain of divorce but to minister in its midst. It is to preach the covenant boldly, confront sin lovingly, and embody grace powerfully.

In a world where marriages are crumbling and families are collapsing, the church must stand as the last sanctuary of hope. Not a museum of perfect marriages, but a hospital for broken ones. Not a courtroom of judgment, but a temple of restoration.

Only then will the church truly reflect her Bridegroom—the One who mends the broken, redeems the fallen, and makes all things new.

CHAPTER 12

QUESTIONS AND OBJECTIONS PEOPLE RAISE ABOUT DIVORCE AND REMARRIAGE

Clarifying Concerns in Light of Scripture

Whenever divorce and remarriage are discussed, questions rise quickly to the surface. They are not theoretical but deeply personal, often born of pain, regret, or fear. Some questions are whispered in tears; others are asked with anger or confusion. The task of the church is not to silence these questions but to answer them with both the truth of Scripture and the compassion of Christ.

MUST I LEAVE MY NEW SPOUSE AND RETURN TO MY FIRST?

One of the most troubling questions believers wrestle with is whether a second marriage, entered after a wrongful divorce, must be dissolved in order to return to the first spouse. Some argue that Jesus' words about remarriage being adultery require such a return. But Scripture speaks differently.

Deuteronomy 24:1–4 clearly forbids a divorced woman who has married another man from going back to her first husband. To break a second covenant in an attempt to restore the first is not obedience but a compounding of sin. The path of redemption is not endless breaking of vows, but repentance and consecration in the covenant you are now in. If a remarriage began wrongly, repentance is needed–but once a covenant exists, it must be honored.

IS ABUSE A BIBLICAL GROUND FOR DIVORCE?

The Bible does not list "abuse" as a category in the way it lists adultery or abandonment, yet the heart of God leaves no doubt. Malachi 2:16 speaks of husbands who "cover their garments with violence" toward their wives. Paul commands husbands to love their wives as their own bodies, never to be harsh (Eph. 5:28–29; Col. 3:19). Abuse is not a minor failing; it is covenant treachery.

Whether physical, verbal, or emotional, abuse destroys the very essence of marriage. It is a form of abandonment in spirit, even if not in body. A spouse who uses covenant as a license to torment has already broken covenant. The abused are not called to remain enslaved. God has called us to peace.

WHAT IF I DIVORCED BEFORE SALVATION?

This question weighs heavily on many who come to Christ later in life. "Am I forever bound by the mistakes of my past? Does God see me as unclean because of what I did before I knew Him?"

The gospel gives a clear answer: *No.* Paul declares, "If anyone is in Christ, he is a new creation. The old has passed away; behold, the new has come" (2 Cor. 5:17). Past divorces, however painful, are covered by the blood of Christ. You are not chained to your pre-salvation story. You are free to live as a new creation, building a covenant that honors Christ today.

WHAT IF I WAS THE GUILTY PARTY?

Another question is asked with trembling: "I was the one who committed adultery, who abandoned, who filed for divorce without cause. Am I forever excluded from grace?"

The answer again is no. Adultery is a grievous sin, but it is not the unforgivable sin. David committed adultery and murder, yet through repentance was restored. If you were the guilty party, repentance is the door to redemption. You may not erase the past, but you can be forgiven, cleansed, and empowered to walk faithfully from this day forward.

DOES GOD EVER COMMAND DIVORCE?

This seems almost unthinkable, but in Ezra 10, God commanded Israel to put away pagan wives who were leading them into idolatry. This was not a casual divorce but a radical act of covenant protection. It shows that while divorce grieves God's heart, there are times when separation serves the higher purpose of guarding His people's holiness.

This passage reminds us that the ultimate covenant is with God Himself. If any human relationship draws us into covenant-breaking with Him, that relationship must be surrendered.

SHOULD I WAIT FOREVER FOR AN ABSENT SPOUSE?

Some abandoned spouses live in limbo, wondering if faithfulness requires waiting indefinitely for the one who left. Paul answers: "If the unbelieving partner separates, let it be so. In such cases the brother or sister is not enslaved. God has called you to peace" (1 Cor. 7:15).

Faithfulness does not mean indefinite captivity. If reconciliation is possible, it should be pursued. But if abandonment is final, the believer is not bound forever to a broken vow. God's desire is not bondage, but peace.

DID I CAUSE MY PARENTS' DIVORCE?

This is a question not often spoken but silently carried in countless young hearts. Children of divorce often blame themselves: "If I had behaved better, if I hadn't caused stress, maybe they would have stayed together."

The truth must be declared loudly: children do not cause divorce. Adults break covenant; children are never the cause. To every hurting son or daughter, the Word of God speaks comfort: "Though my father and mother forsake me, the Lord will take me in" (Ps. 27:10). God Himself steps in as Father for the forsaken.

DOES DIVORCE KEEP ME OUT OF HEAVEN?

Some live in fear that divorce has forever excluded them from God's kingdom. Yet Scripture is clear: what separates us from heaven is not divorce but unrepented sin and unbelief. Divorce is a sin when outside of God's will, but it is not the unpardonable sin.

The thief on the cross had no opportunity to fix his past, yet Jesus promised him Paradise because he turned in faith. In the same way, those scarred by divorce can be washed, cleansed, and welcomed into the eternal embrace of Christ.

CONCLUSION: GRACE GREATER THAN OUR QUESTIONS

These questions are many, and the answers are not always simple. Yet through them all runs a thread of truth: marriage is sacred, divorce is grievous, but grace is greater. The church must hold covenant high but must also lift grace higher still. We must be the people who do not shy away from the hard questions but meet them with both Scripture and compassion.

In the end, every question about divorce and remarriage points us to the cross — where covenant was broken by humanity yet restored by Christ; where sin abounded, but grace abounded more.

CHAPTER 13

HEALING AFTER DIVORCE: PERSONAL, SPIRITUAL, AND RELATIONAL RENEWAL

Hope Restored

Divorce leaves deep wounds. It is not just a legal matter or a relational shift but a tearing of covenant that affects spirit, soul, and body. Even when a divorce was necessary—for reasons of abuse, abandonment, or betrayal—the pain lingers like an echo. Some describe it as death without a funeral: the loss is real, but closure is elusive. Yet the God we serve is not only a God of truth but also a God of healing. He binds up the brokenhearted, He restores the years the locusts have eaten, and He makes all things new.

Healing after divorce is possible. It does not happen overnight, but it is the work of grace over time. In this chapter, we will walk through the journey of personal renewal, spiritual restoration, and relational rebuilding for those who have been wounded by divorce.

PERSONAL HEALING: FACING THE WOUND HONESTLY

The first step toward healing is honesty. Too often, divorced believers try to minimize their pain: "I'm fine. It wasn't that bad. I just need to move on." But unacknowledged wounds fester. Psalm 34:18 says, "The Lord is near to the brokenhearted and saves the crushed in spirit." God does not heal what we refuse to bring into the light.

Personal healing requires grieving what was lost: the marriage that failed, the dreams that died, and the stability that vanished. Grieving does not mean living in despair; it means giving sorrow its voice so it can be released. Like the psalmists who poured out their laments before God, divorced believers must cry out their pain. Healing begins when pretense ends.

Illustration

A woman once told me, "I never allowed myself to cry after my divorce. I thought it was weakness. But the day I wept before God, I felt His arms wrap around me for the first time in years." Tears are not failure; they are the doorway to comfort.

SPIRITUAL HEALING: BREAKING SHAME AND GUILT

Divorce carries not only pain but also shame. Many believers feel like second-class Christians, convinced they wear a scarlet letter in the eyes of others and even of God. Yet the gospel speaks a different word. Romans 8:1 declares, "There is therefore now no condemnation for those who are in Christ Jesus."

Spiritual healing means breaking the lie that divorce defines you. Your identity is not "divorced." Your identity is child of God, beloved, redeemed. Divorce may be part of your story, but it is not your name. When Jesus encountered the Samaritan woman at the well–a woman with five failed marriages–He did not call her "divorced." He called her to be a worshiper in spirit and truth, and He sent her as an evangelist to her city. He rewrote her identity in grace.

For some, spiritual healing also requires renouncing curses spoken over words like "you'll never be loved again" or "you'll always be broken." These are lies from the enemy. The blood of Christ speaks louder, declaring freedom and newness.

RELATIONAL HEALING: FORGIVENESS AND RECONCILIATION

Relational healing is often the hardest. Divorce creates bitterness. Former spouses carry resentment, sometimes justifiably so. Yet bitterness chains the heart long after papers are signed. Healing requires forgiveness.

Forgiveness does not mean excusing what happened. It does not mean forgetting or reconciling if the other party remains unrepentant. Forgiveness is releasing debt, choosing not to carry poison in your own soul. Ephesians 4:31–32 calls us to "let all bitterness and wrath… be put away," and to forgive as God in Christ forgave us.

Relational healing may also extend to children, in-laws, and friends caught in the fallout. Divorce often divides not only couples but entire communities. Healing requires intentional rebuilding–showing children they are loved, refusing to poison them with bitterness, and learning to co-parent with civility even when love is gone.

CASE STUDY

I once counseled a father who had not spoken to his ex-wife in years, except through lawyers. Their daughter was caught in the middle. Over time, he chose to forgive, not to restore the marriage, but to restore peace for their child. His ex-wife never repented, but he stopped carrying hatred. Their daughter later testified, "I saw Jesus in my dad because he chose love over bitterness."

REBUILDING TRUST WITH GOD AND WITH SELF

One of the hidden wounds of divorce is loss of self-trust. Many wonder, "How could I have chosen so badly? How did I not see the signs? Can I ever trust my own judgment again?" This self-doubt often bleeds into their walk with God: "Didn't God warn me? Did I miss His voice?"

Healing here requires a rediscovery of God's faithfulness. Even when we make poor choices, God is able to redeem. Romans 8:28 promises that all things, even failed marriages, work together for good for those who love Him. Divorce is not the end of your story; it can be the soil where God grows new strength, new wisdom, and new compassion.

Learning to trust yourself again comes slowly. It begins by anchoring your identity in Christ rather than in past decisions. It matures through community–allowing trusted pastors, mentors, and spiritual friends to walk with you. Over time, trust is rebuilt not by perfection but by grace.

THE ROLE OF THE CHURCH IN HEALING

Healing after divorce is rarely accomplished alone. The church must be a restoration community. This means offering support groups for divorced believers, counseling resources, intercessory prayer, and a culture of grace rather than judgment. The church should be the place where those scared by divorce find hope, not shame.

Imagine a congregation where a divorced woman is not whispered about but embraced, where a single father is not pitied but strengthened, where children of divorce are surrounded by spiritual aunts, uncles, and grandparents who fill the gaps. That is what the healing church looks like.

PROPHETIC RESTORATION: A NEW BEGINNING

God is a Redeemer. He does not merely patch up wounds; He makes all things new. Joel 2:25 carries a prophetic promise: "I will restore to you the years that the swarming locust has eaten." Divorce may have devoured years, dreams, and joy–but God can restore. For some, that restoration may mean remarriage in the Lord. For others, it may mean flourishing in singleness. For all, it means peace, wholeness, and a future filled with hope.

ILLUSTRATION

A woman once told me, "After my divorce, I thought my life was over. But God met me in my loneliness, and He became my husband. Years later, He gave me a new marriage, but the greatest gift was not my new husband–it was the intimacy I found with Him in the wilderness."

CLOSING REFLECTION

Divorce is devastating, but it is not the end. Healing is possible–personal healing through honest grief, spiritual healing through breaking shame, relational healing through forgiveness, and prophetic healing through restoration. The journey is long, but the destination is peaceful.

The God who hates divorce is also the God who heals the divorced. He hates the tearing, but He loves the torn. He despises the betrayal, but He restores the betrayed. In Christ, every scar can become a testimony, every wound a witness, and every broken covenant an altar of grace.

CHAPTER 14

Rebuilding Life and Purpose After Divorce

"Finding Meaning Beyond the Pain

Divorce has a way of leaving people feeling like life itself has collapsed. For many, it is not only the loss of a spouse but also the shattering of dreams, the dismantling of stability, and the silencing of hope. The vows once spoken with trembling joy now echo as reminders of disappointment. For some, even the thought of rebuilding feels impossible. Yet the God we serve is not only the God of covenant but also the God of restoration. He is the One who brings beauty from ashes, joy from mourning, and life from what seems to be death.

In the midst of the chaos and heartache of divorce, it can be difficult to see a way forward. But as we lean on our faith and trust in God's promises, we can find the strength to take each step towards healing and wholeness. It may not be easy, and the road ahead may be long and challenging, but we can hold onto the hope that God is with us every step of the way, guiding us towards a future filled with redemption and renewal. With His grace and love, we can find peace in the midst of the storm and begin to see glimpses of a new beginning emerging from the ruins of our brokenness.

When divorce strikes, it is tempting to believe the story is over. The enemy whispers lies: "You are finished. You are disqualified. You will never rise again." But the voice of God speaks differently: "Behold, I make all things new." This chapter is for those who wonder how to start again. It is not a list of cold instructions but a testimony of God's redeeming grace that still flows, even after broken covenants. It is a reminder that even in the darkest moments, there is always hope for a brighter tomorrow. God's love is never-ending, and His plans for us are always good, even when we can't see it in the midst of our pain. So take heart, dear friend, for this is not the end of your story. It is the beginning of a new chapter filled with healing, restoration, and the promise of a beautiful future ahead.

REDISCOVERING WHO YOU ARE

The first step in rebuilding is rediscovering identity. Divorce has a way of reshaping how a person sees themselves. Some feel marked forever: divorced, abandoned, unworthy. Yet God never renames His children by their failures. He calls them beloved, chosen, and redeemed.

In order to move forward and embrace the new chapter ahead, it is crucial to reconnect with the truth of who you are in God's eyes. Take the time to reflect on your worth and value, not based on your past mistakes or circumstances, but on the unconditional love and grace that God offers. Remember that you are a cherished child of God, deserving of love, forgiveness, and a bright future. Embrace this truth and allow it to guide you as you navigate the journey of healing and restoration.

As you begin to internalize this truth, you will find strength and courage to let go of the shame and guilt that may have been weighing you down. Allow yourself to fully accept God's forgiveness and embrace the freedom that comes with it. Trust in His plan for your life and believe that He has a purpose for you, despite any setbacks or failures you may have experienced. With God's love as your foundation, you can move forward with confidence and hope, knowing that you are never alone in your journey towards healing and restoration.

FULLY ACCEPTED, FOREVER LOVED

Remember that God's love is unconditional and His grace is always available to you. Take comfort in the fact that He is always ready to welcome you back with open arms, no matter how far you may have strayed. Let go of any feelings of unworthiness or inadequacy and instead focus on the truth that you are a beloved child of God. Embrace the truth that you are worthy of love and forgiveness and allow yourself to experience the peace and joy that come from being in His presence. Trust in His promises and lean on His strength as you continue your journey of healing and restoration.

Remember that God's grace is not based on our own merit or deserving, but on His unconditional love for us. As you surrender your fears and doubts to Him, He will replace them with His peace and reassurance. Allow yourself to be filled with His love and let it overflow into every aspect of your life. Embrace the freedom that comes from knowing that you are fully accepted and cherished by the One who created you. Let His grace be your guide as you navigate the challenges and uncertainties of life, knowing that He is always by your side, ready to support and uplift you.

His love knows no bounds and His grace is sufficient for all your needs. Trust in His plan for your life and lean on Him in times of trouble. With God as your foundation, you can weather any storm and overcome any obstacle. Take comfort in the knowledge that you are never alone, for He is always with you, guiding you and holding you in His loving embrace. Let His love transform you from the inside out, shaping you into the person He created you to be. Walk in His light and let His love shine through you, illuminating the darkness and bringing hope to those around you.

DEFINED BY CHRIST, NOT BY FAILURE

Paul's words in 2 Corinthians 5:17 speak loudly here: "If anyone is in Christ, he is a new creation. The old has passed away; behold, the new has come." Notice the Scripture does not say, "If anyone has a perfect marriage…" or "If anyone has never failed…" but rather, "If anyone is in Christ." Your covenant with God is unbroken, even when human covenants fail.

Therefore, as a new creation in Christ, you are called to reflect His love and grace in all areas of your life, including your relationships. Even when faced with challenges or failures, remember that God's love for you is constant and unwavering. Let this truth guide you as you navigate the complexities of human relationships, knowing that you are ultimately defined by your identity in Christ. Embrace this new creation reality and allow it to shape how you approach every aspect of your life, including your marriage and other relationships. Trust in God's faithfulness and rely on His strength to help you walk in His light and love, even in the midst of darkness and struggles.

Remember that God's love is the foundation upon which you can build healthy and thriving relationships with others. As you lean on His grace and guidance, you will find the strength and wisdom to navigate the ups and downs of life with a spirit of love and forgiveness. Let your relationships be a reflection of God's love and grace and watch as He transforms them into sources of joy, peace, and fulfillment. Trust in His plan for your life and rest in the knowledge that His love will always sustain you, no matter what challenges may come your way. Proverbs 3:5-6 reminds us to trust in the Lord with all our hearts and lean not on our own understanding. In all our ways, we are to acknowledge Him, and He will direct our paths. Trusting in God's love and guidance will lead us to fulfilling relationships and a life filled with peace and joy. Let us put our faith in Him, knowing that His love will always sustain us through any trials we may face.

As we continue to walk in faith and trust in God's plan for our lives, we can be confident that He will never leave us nor forsake us. Even in the midst of uncertainty and challenges, His love remains constant and unwavering. By surrendering our fears and worries to Him, we can experience a sense of peace that surpasses all understanding. Let us hold fast to the promises of God and allow His love to guide us through every season of life.

TESTIMONY

I once counseled a man who said, "I no longer know who I am. I was a husband, and now I am nothing." Through tears, we opened the Word and saw that his true identity was not in being a husband but in being a son of God. Slowly, he began to rebuild, not as a failure, but as a forgiven child of the King.

As he embraced this truth, his confidence and sense of purpose were restored. He realized that his worth was not dependent on his past mistakes or current circumstances, but on the unconditional love and grace of his Heavenly Father. With each step forward, he grew stronger in his faith and more secure in his identity as a beloved child of God. The journey was not easy, but he found comfort in knowing that he was never alone, for God was always by his side, guiding and strengthening him along the way. And as he continued to trust in God's promises and lean on His unfailing love, he discovered a newfound sense of peace and purpose that filled his heart with joy and gratitude.

REBUILDING DAILY LIFE

After the storm of divorce, many feel paralyzed. The daily rhythms of life such as eating, resting and working–become heavy burdens. Some drown themselves in busyness to escape the pain; others withdraw and neglect themselves.

But for those who turn to God for healing and restoration, there is hope. Just as He helped the man in his journey through the wilderness, God can also guide and strengthen those rebuilding their lives after divorce. With faith and perseverance, they can find a new sense of purpose and joy, allowing them to move forward with confidence and trust in God's plan for their future. By leaning on His unfailing love and trusting in His promises, they can experience a peace that surpasses all understanding, even in the midst of their pain and struggles.

Rebuilding begins with small steps of life-giving discipline. Prayer and seeking guidance from a trusted spiritual counselor can provide direction and support along the way. Setting boundaries, establishing healthy routines, and surrounding oneself with positive influences can also aid in the healing process. By prioritizing self-care and focusing on personal growth, individuals can gradually rebuild their sense of self-worth and resilience. Taking each day one step at a time, with faith as their foundation, those navigating life after divorce can find hope and restoration in God's grace.

Take time to breathe. Remember to be gentle with yourself and allow yourself to feel all the emotions that come with this difficult journey. It's important to practice self-compassion and forgiveness, both towards yourself and towards your ex-partner. By taking time to breathe and reflect on your progress, you can continue to move forward towards healing and renewal. Trust that with time and patience, you will emerge from this challenging chapter of your life stronger and more resilient than before. Reestablish rhythms of prayer, rest, and nourishment for your soul. Surround yourself with supportive loved ones who can provide comfort and encouragement as you navigate through this season of healing. Remember that healing is a process, and it's okay to take things one day at a time. By reestablishing routines that nurture your spiritual, emotional, and physical well-being, you can gradually find peace and wholeness in the midst of your pain. Trust that God's grace is sufficient to carry you through this time of transition and renewal. Keep the faith and believe that brighter days are ahead. Care for your body, because it remains the temple of the Holy Spirit. Begin to dream again of things you once loved. What seem like little steps are seeds of restoration.

These small actions will eventually blossom into a renewed sense of purpose and joy. Remember to be patient with yourself as you navigate this healing journey. Surround yourself with supportive friends and family who can offer encouragement and love. Seek out professional help if needed, whether that be through therapy, counseling, or support groups. You are not alone in this process, and there is always hope for a brighter tomorrow. Keep moving forward, one step at a time, knowing that you are deserving of peace and happiness.

I recall a woman who, after decades in a loveless and broken marriage, finally found herself free yet empty. "I don't even know what I like anymore," she confessed. God led her to take a painting class–something she had always wanted but had suppressed for years. With every stroke of color, her soul began to heal. God used a simple brush and canvas to awaken the truth that life was not over.

It was just beginning. As she painted, she rediscovered parts of herself that had long been buried beneath the weight of disappointment and regret. Each piece of art she created was a reflection of her innermost thoughts and feelings, a visual representation of her journey towards self-discovery and renewal. With each stroke of the brush, she found a sense of purpose and fulfillment that had been missing for so long. Painting became her therapy, her outlet for expression, and her pathway to healing. As she stood back and admired her work, she realized that she was not just creating art, but she was creating a new life for herself, one filled with color, beauty, and endless possibilities.

REBUILDING FAMILY

Children are often the silent victims of divorce. They rarely cause the split, yet they always carry its weight.

The impact of divorce on children can be profound, leaving them feeling confused, hurt, and abandoned. As parents navigate the complexities of co-parenting and adjusting to their new lives, it is essential to prioritize the well-being of their children. Building a strong and supportive family dynamic post-divorce requires open communication, empathy, and a commitment to putting the needs of the children first. By creating a sense of stability, consistency, and love, parents can help their children navigate the challenges of divorce and thrive in their new family dynamic. It is a journey of rebuilding trust, resilience, and connection, but with dedication and effort, families can come out stronger and more united on the other side.

To rebuild purpose after divorce is to look into the eyes of sons and daughters and remind them, "This is not your fault. You are loved. We will make it through this together."

It is important for parents to communicate openly and honestly with their children, reassuring them that they are not to blame for the divorce and that they are still loved unconditionally. Building a strong support system for both the parents and the children can also help in navigating the emotional challenges that come with divorce. By seeking therapy, joining support groups, and leaning on friends and family for support, families can find the strength to heal and move forward in a positive direction. With time, patience, and a willingness to work together, families can create a new sense of purpose and unity after divorce.

Parents must resist the temptation to weaponize children against one another. The call of God is to shield them, not scar them further. Divorce may have fractured the marriage, but it does not have to destroy the family. A new kind of family rhythm can be built—one anchored not in bitterness but in the peace of Christ.

This new rhythm may require setting aside personal grievances and focusing on the well-being of the children. It may involve creating new traditions and routines that foster a sense of stability and security. It may also mean seeking professional help or counseling to navigate the challenges of co-parenting and rebuilding trust. Ultimately, the goal is to create a safe and loving environment where children can thrive despite the changes that come with divorce. By prioritizing the needs of the family as a whole and committing to a process of healing and growth, families can emerge from divorce stronger and more resilient than before.

Psalm 27:10 says, "Though my father and mother forsake me, the Lord will take me in." When children see parents leaning on the Lord for healing, they learn that brokenness is not the end. They see grace at work and find courage for their own futures.

REBUILDING FINANCES

Few things shake a life after divorce as much as finances. For many, divorce brings debt, division of assets, or even poverty. The shame of financial ruin adds weight to emotional pain. Yet Scripture reminds us that the God who fed Elijah by ravens and sustained the widow of Zarephath can also sustain His children in seasons of loss.

This provision may come in unexpected ways, such as through a new job opportunity, a community rallying around with support, or even a sense of peace and contentment in simplicity. Trusting in God's provision allows individuals to let go of the worry and fear that often accompany financial struggles after divorce. It is a reminder that God is faithful and will never abandon His children, even in their darkest moments.

Rebuilding purpose includes learning new stewardship, new creativity, and new trust in God's provision. For some, this may mean budgeting for the first time. For others, it may mean stepping into entrepreneurship, retraining for a new career, or simply learning to live within new means with contentment.

Regardless of the specific path chosen, rebuilding purpose after divorce is a journey of self-discovery and growth. It requires resilience, determination, and a willingness to embrace change. It is an opportunity to redefine one's identity, priorities, and goals. As individuals navigate this new chapter of their lives, they may find unexpected blessings and opportunities for personal and spiritual growth. Trusting in God's provision can be a source of strength and comfort during this challenging time. One scripture that can provide comfort during this challenging time of rebuilding after divorce is Philippians 4:19, "And my God shall supply all your need according to His riches in glory by Christ Jesus." This verse reminds us that God is our ultimate provider and will meet all our needs as we journey through this period of transition. Trusting in His provision can give us the strength and peace we need to move forward with confidence and hope.

By leaning on their faith and seeking support from loved ones, individuals can find the courage to face the unknown with grace and resilience. It is a time to reflect on past mistakes and learn from them, while also looking towards the future with hope and optimism. Through this process of rebuilding, individuals can discover a newfound sense of purpose and fulfillment that can ultimately lead to a more fulfilling and meaningful life post-divorce.

It is important to remember that healing takes time and patience, and it is okay to seek professional help if needed. Surrounding oneself with positive influences and engaging in self-care activities can also aid in the healing process. By taking things one day at a time and focusing on personal growth, individuals can emerge from this challenging period stronger and more resilient than ever before.

TESTIMONY

One brother told me, "Divorce took my savings, my house, and half my income. But it gave me a new trust in Jehovah Jireh. For the first time, I know God truly provides." What the enemy meant for evil, God used as a school of faith.

This brother's story serves as a powerful reminder that even in the midst of hardship and loss, there is always an opportunity for growth and spiritual transformation. Through the trials and tribulations of divorce, he was able to deepen his faith and trust in God, finding solace in the belief that God's plan is greater than any setback or struggle. This newfound perspective allowed him to see the silver lining in a difficult situation, ultimately leading to a sense of peace and resilience that he may not have discovered otherwise. In times of adversity, it is important to remember that there is always potential for growth and renewal, even in the darkest of times. Trusting in God and embracing the lessons that come from challenging experiences can ultimately lead to a greater sense of purpose and strength in the face of adversity.

REBUILDING CALLING AND MINISTRY

Perhaps the deepest wound of divorce is the belief that God is finished with you. Many divorced believers feel disqualified, "I can never minister again. I can never serve again." But Scripture tells a different story.

In fact, some of the greatest leaders in the Bible faced their own trials and setbacks, only to rise again with a renewed sense of calling and purpose. Just as Job experienced great loss and suffering, only to be restored and blessed even more abundantly, those who have gone through divorce can also find redemption and restoration in God's plan for their lives. It is through these difficult times that our faith is tested and refined, ultimately leading us to a deeper understanding of God's grace and love for us. So, instead of seeing divorce as the end of your ministry, see it as an opportunity for God to rebuild and reshape your calling in a way that is even more powerful and impactful than before. Trust in God's plan for your life and allow Him to use your story of redemption and restoration to bring hope and healing to others who may be going through similar struggles.

Moses was a murderer, yet God made him a deliverer. In the same way, God can take our brokenness and turn it into something beautiful. He can use our past mistakes and failures to bring about His redemption and restoration in our lives. Just as He did with Moses, He can take what was meant for harm and use it for good. Trust in His plan and have faith that He can turn your story of brokenness into a testimony of His grace and love.

David committed adultery, yet God restored him as a man after His own heart. No matter how far we may have fallen or how broken we may feel, God's grace is always there to lift us up and transform us. Just like He did with David, He can turn our deepest regrets and sins into opportunities for growth and renewal. Let us trust in His unfailing love and have faith that He can make something beautiful out of our brokenness.

The Samaritan woman, with five failed marriages, became one of the first evangelists of the New Testament. If God could use them, He can still use you.

FROM WEAKNESS TO WITNESS

Let us surrender our past mistakes and weaknesses to Him, knowing that His power is made perfect in our weaknesses. Just as He used Moses, David, and the Samaritan woman, He can use us to spread His love and grace to others. Let us have faith that through God's transformative power, we can be a beacon of hope and redemption to those around us.

Just as God used these flawed individuals for His greater purpose, He can also use your brokenness and pain to bring about something beautiful. Embrace the journey of healing and transformation, knowing that God's grace is more than sufficient to carry you through. Let go of any shame or guilt, and allow God to work in and through you, creating a testimony of His faithfulness and redemption. Trust in His timing and His perfect plan for your life, knowing that He is always at work, even in the midst of your darkest moments.

The Bible is full of tales of flawed people whom God used in amazing ways. Your past mistakes do not define you but rather serve as a testimony to God's ability to bring beauty from ashes. Embrace the journey of healing and restoration, knowing that God can use even the most broken parts of your story for His glory. Trust in His unfailing love and grace and allow Him to turn your pain into a powerful testimony of His faithfulness. "For I am persuaded that neither death nor life, nor angels nor principalities nor powers, nor things present nor things to come, nor height nor depth, nor any other created thing, shall be able to separate us from the love of God which is in Christ Jesus our Lord." – Romans 8:38-39

In every season of life, remember that God's love and grace are always present. Trust in His plan and know that He can use your past mistakes for His glory. Embrace the journey of healing and restoration, allowing God to turn your pain into a powerful testimony of His faithfulness.

God's gifts are without repentance (Romans 11:29). That means they are not withdrawn because of failure. When repented of, forgiven, and consecrated, your life becomes a testimony that broken vessels still pour out oil.

As you walk in the light of God's love and grace, remember that He is always with you, guiding you through every trial and triumph. Your past does not define you but rather serves as a stepping stone towards a brighter future in Him. Embrace the journey of transformation and allow God to mold you into a vessel of His glory, shining His light through your brokenness. Trust in His unfailing love and know that He is faithful to complete the good work He has started in you (Philippians 1:6).

REBUILDING COMMUNITY

Divorce isolates individuals and families, leaving them feeling alone and disconnected. However, by coming together in a spirit of love and acceptance, we can break down those barriers and rebuild a sense of community. Through support and encouragement, we can help each other through the difficult times and ultimately find healing and restoration. Let us not be defined by our past mistakes but instead focus on the love and grace that God offers us, knowing that we are never alone in our journey towards a brighter future.

Friends choose sides, churches sometimes withdraw, and loneliness becomes a heavy chain. Yet rebuilding requires community. It requires daring to walk into fellowship again, daring to trust again, and daring to be vulnerable again.

Ecclesiastes 4:9–10 says, "Two are better than one… for if they fall, one will lift up his fellow." You need people who will lift you up when you fall, who will remind you of who you are in Christ, and who will walk with you as you rebuild.

Rebuilding community and fellowship and drawing those who are divorced closer to fellowship is important so that they don't feel rejected. Creating a safe and welcoming space for those who have experienced divorce is essential in rebuilding community. By showing love and compassion, we can help individuals see that their worth is not defined by their past relationships. Let us come together to support and uplift one another, knowing that God's love is always present, guiding us towards a future filled with hope and healing.

Let us be the hands and feet of Christ, extending grace and understanding to all who are in need of restoration and connection. "For those who have no sin, let them throw the first stone" (John 8:7). It is through this message of forgiveness and grace that we can come together in fellowship, accepting one another without judgment. Let us create a community where all are welcomed and valued, regardless of their past mistakes. In doing so, we can help each other heal and grow, knowing that God's love is always there to guide us towards a brighter future. Together, we can support one another and lift each other up, knowing that God's love and grace are always present. By rebuilding community and fostering a spirit of unity and acceptance, we can create a safe space for healing and growth. Let us come together in faith and love, trusting in God's plan for restoration and renewal in our lives and relationships.

PROPHETIC VISION FOR THE FUTURE

Rebuilding life and purpose is not about going back to what was lost – it is about stepping into what is new. God does not simply restore what was; He multiplies. Joel 2:25 is not just a poetic promise but a prophetic decree: "I will restore to you the years that the swarming locust has eaten."

As we move forward with faith and hope, we can envision a future filled with abundance and blessings beyond what we can imagine. This prophetic vision for the future is one of restoration, renewal, and redemption. It is a vision of God's faithfulness and provision, as He promises to not only restore what was lost but to multiply it in ways that exceed our wildest dreams. Let us hold onto this vision as we journey towards healing and wholeness, trusting in God's perfect timing and plan for our lives.

Restoration does not mean "replacing the old with the same." It means new harvest, new relationships, new dreams, and new joy. Your latter years can be greater than your former. As we walk in faith and obedience, God will bring about a transformation in our lives that will far surpass anything we could have ever imagined. The restoration He offers is not merely a patch-up job but a complete overhaul that brings about new beginnings and opportunities. Let us embrace this vision of restoration with hope and expectancy, knowing that God's promises are true and His blessings are abundant. May we look forward to the future with confidence, knowing that God is faithful to fulfill all He has spoken over our lives. "For I will restore health to you and heal you of your wounds, says the Lord." – Jeremiah 30:17 (NKJV)

In times of difficulty and brokenness, it is comforting to know that God promises restoration and healing to those who trust in Him. No matter what we have gone through, God has the power to bring about a new season of blessing and abundance in our lives. Let us hold on to this promise, believing that God's restoration is not only possible, but inevitable for those who place their faith in Him.

TESTIMONY

I once heard a man pray after his divorce, "Lord, let me live again before I die." God answered by giving him not only peace but also a new purpose–he began mentoring young men in his church, pouring into them the wisdom bought through pain. His tears became seeds of transformation for others.

May we also have the faith to believe that God can bring beauty from our brokenness, and that He can use our struggles to bring hope and healing to those around us. Just as this man found a new purpose and calling in his season of loss, may we too trust that God has a plan to redeem and restore every part of our lives. Let us hold fast to the promise that God is always working for our good, even in the midst of our darkest moments.

FINAL WORD

Divorce may have ended a marriage, but it does not end your life, your calling, or your story. The God of covenant is also the God of new beginnings. He who raised Jesus from the dead can raise your life from the ashes.

Just as the man in the story found a new purpose and calling after his loss, we too can trust that God has a plan to redeem and restore every part of our lives. We must hold fast to the promise that God is always working for our good, even in the midst of our darkest moments. Divorce may have ended a marriage, but it does not define us. Our calling and our story are not over. The God of covenant is also the God of new beginnings, capable of raising our lives from the ashes just as he raised Jesus from the dead.

So, rise again. Dream again. Love again. Serve again. For your God is still with you, your covenant with Him remains unbroken, and your future is not behind you but before you. Take heart and have faith, for the trials and tribulations of this world are temporary, but the love and mercy of God are eternal. Embrace the journey ahead with hope and courage, knowing that God is always by your side, guiding you towards a brighter tomorrow. Keep your eyes fixed on the promises of God, for He is faithful and will never abandon you. Trust in His plan for your life and believe that He will turn your mourning into dancing and your sorrow into joy. Rise up, child of God, and walk in the light of His grace, for your best days are yet to come.

PART IV

Closing Word

CONCLUSION

FROM ASHES TO BEAUTY

THIS BOOK HAS BEEN ONE of the most difficult I have ever written. The subject of divorce and remarriage touches some of the deepest wounds in human life. It carries with it pain, confusion, guilt, and even shame. I have walked carefully, with the fear of God, because these are not just theological debates but real lives, real tears, and real families.

Let me be absolutely clear: the purpose of this book is not to encourage divorce. It is not to open a door for people to escape covenant lightly or to offer excuses for selfishness. God's heart is always for covenant, always for restoration, and always for reconciliation wherever possible. From the beginning, it was not so that marriages should be broken. Divorce grieves God's heart because it shatters the covenant He designed to reflect His own love for His people.

Yet, as a pastor and a shepherd, I could not ignore the reality that many of God's children are suffering—not always because of rebellion, but often because of ignorance. Too many have lived in confusion, uncertain of what the Scriptures truly teach. Too many have been crushed under condemnation, believing themselves forever disqualified because of past failures. Too many have endured abuse and treachery in silence, told that to speak up would be to dishonor God, when in fact God Himself had already declared, "I have called you to peace."

If you have walked this painful road, I want to say from my heart: I am sorry. Sorry that the church has often spoken more words of judgment than of healing. Sorry that silence has sometimes replaced shepherding, and shame has replaced compassion. Sorry that you have been left to carry burdens that Christ Himself came to lift.

This book was written for you and not to trivialize covenant, but to honor it rightly; not to make excuses for sin, but to magnify the grace of God that redeems sinners; not to close the door of ministry, but to open the door of restoration. My prayer is that through these pages, the truth of Scripture has brought clarity, and the Spirit of God has whispered hope.

Divorce is never the end of God's story. Even in the ashes, He is at work. He restores the years the locusts have eaten. He heals the brokenhearted. He gives beauty for ashes, the oil of joy for mourning, and the garment of praise for the spirit of heaviness (Isa. 61:3). He makes streams flow in deserts and brings resurrection out of death.

If you are married, may this book call you to guard your covenant fiercely. If you are divorced, may it remind you that you are not beyond grace. If you are remarried, may it guide you to honor the covenant you now stand in with holiness. If you are a leader, may it equip you to shepherd the flock of God with truth and compassion.

Above all, may this book leave you with hope. Hope that failure is not final. Hope that scars can become testimonies. Hope that your story, however broken, can become an altar of God's redemptive power.

From covenant to brokenness, and from brokenness back to covenant–

this is the journey of grace. May the God who keeps covenant, who restores marriages, who heals wounds, and who redeems stories, take your ashes and make them beautiful.

Dr. Jean Héder Petit Frère

Afterword

A PROPHETIC PRAYER AND CHARGE

Beloved of the Lord, if you have walked through the pages of this book, you have walked through valleys and mountains. You have faced the pain of broken covenants and the hope of restoration. You have seen the seriousness of marriage, the tragedy of divorce, and the power of God's redeeming grace. Now, as you close these pages, I do not want you to simply close a book—I want you to open your heart to the Spirit of God who makes all things new.

I release this prophetic charge over you: **Your past does not define you. Your scars are not your name. Your failures are not your destiny.** In Christ, you are not labeled by divorce, by betrayal, by abandonment, or by shame. You are named by covenant: beloved, chosen, redeemed, and restored.

I call you now to rise from the ashes and rebuild. Rebuild your life upon the Rock who cannot be shaken. Rebuild your family altar with prayer, worship, and the Word. Rebuild your identity not on the wreckage of yesterday but on the promises of God that are yes and amen in Christ Jesus.

If you are married, guard your covenant with holy fear and passionate love. If you are divorced, walk in the freedom of forgiveness and the hope of restoration. If you are remarried, honor the covenant you now stand in with faithfulness and grace. And if you are called to walk single for a season, do so with joy, knowing that you are complete in Him.

And now I pray over you: *Father, in the name of Jesus, I lift up every reader of this book. Where there has been pain, bring healing. Where there has been shame, release grace. Where there has been confusion, bring clarity. Where there has been loss, restore with abundance. I break the power of every generational curse, every altar of brokenness, and every lie of the enemy, and I declare freedom in Christ. I release peace into homes, restoration into marriages, and hope into hearts. Lord, raise up a generation who will honor covenant, who will rebuild families, and who will transform nations. Let every scar become a testimony and every broken covenant become an altar of Your redeeming power. In Jesus' mighty name, amen.*

Go now in the strength of the Lord. Build, rebuild, and restore. For your story is not over. God is writing a new chapter—and in His hands, your ashes will become beauty.

ABOUT THE AUTHOR

Dr. Jean Héder Petit Frère is a pastor, visionary, author, and Kingdom ambassador with over 30 years of ministry experience. He is the founder of *Centre Diplomatique Famille Tabernacle de Louange* (CDFTL) and Jubilee Christian Academy in Haiti and the visionary leader of Kingdom Leadership Institute, a ministerial school dedicated to raising and equipping leaders for the nations.

A prolific writer and teacher, Dr. Héder, has authored multiple books on kingdom identity, leadership, and spiritual transformation. Through his radio and media program *Discovering the Kingdom*, he reaches audiences globally with a message of hope, purpose, and the unshakable reality of God's Kingdom.

Known for his prophetic insight and pastoral heart, Dr. Héder ministers with a unique blend of biblical depth, practical wisdom, and Spirit-led compassion. His life mission is to raise leaders, transform lives, and inspire generations to walk in their God-given destiny.

He is married to Marcia Elaine Petit Frère, and together they have three grown children. They continue to labor for the Kingdom with a vision that spans nations and generations.

OTHER WORKS BY THE AUTHOR

The Manual of an Ambassador of the King

The Judicial Power of Resurrection

The Identity Revolution

The Making of a Father

The Airbnb Shortcut

Blood Brother with Christ (forthcoming)

Grace Beyond Divorce (this volume)

More titles are in development as part of a series designed to help believers walk in Kingdom identity, purpose, and transformation.

References

QuillBot. (2025). *QuillBot Flow*. (Oct 2025 version) [Large Language Model]. Retrieved October 15, 2025, from https://quillbot.com/flow

www.ingramcontent.com/pod-product-compliance
Lightning Source LLC
Chambersburg PA
CBHW072156070526
44585CB00015B/1165